First Workshop on Commonsense Representation and Reasoning (CSRR 2022)

Dublin, Ireland
27 May 2022

ISBN: 978-1-7138-6732-6

Printed from e-media with permission by:

Curran Associates, Inc.
57 Morehouse Lane
Red Hook, NY 12571

CURRAN ASSOCIATES INC. proceedings.com

Some format issues inherent in the e-media version may also appear in this print version.

Printed with permission by Curran Associates, Inc. (2023)

For permission requests, please contact the Association for Computational Linguistics at the address below.

Association for Computational Linguistics
209 N. Eighth Street
Stroudsburg, Pennsylvania 18360

Phone: 1-570-476-8006
Fax: 1-570-476-0860

acl@aclweb.org

Additional copies of this publication are available from:

Curran Associates, Inc.
57 Morehouse Lane
Red Hook, NY 12571 USA
Phone: 845-758-0400
Fax: 845-758-2633
Email: curran@proceedings.com
Web: www.proceedings.com

CSRR 2022

The First Workshop on Commonsense Representation and Reasoning

May 27, 2022

The CSRR organizers gratefully acknowledge the support from the following sponsors.

Gold

Ai2 Allen Institute for AI

Introduction

Welcome to the First Workshop on Commonsense Representation and Reasoning (CSRR 2022)! The workshop was co-located with the 60th Annual Meeting of the Association for Computational Linguistics and was held on May 27, 2022 as a hybrid workshop. The workshop was organised by Antoine Bosselut, Xiang Li, Bill Yuchen Lin, Vered Schwartz, Bodhisattwa Prasad Majumdar, Yash Kumar Lal, Rachel Rudinger, Xiang Ren, Niket Tandon and Vilém Zouhar. We take this opportunity to thank the CSRR 2022 program committee for their help and thorough reviews. We also thank the authors who presented their work at the workshop, and the workshop participants for the valuable feedback and discussions. Finally, we are deeply honored to have excellent talks from our invited speakers.

Organizing Committee

Organizers

Antoine Bosselut, EPFL, Switzerland
Xiang Li, University of Massachusetts, Amherst
Bill Yuchen Lin, University of Southern California
Vered Shwartz, University of British Columbia
Bodhisattwa Prasad Majumder, University of California, San Diego
Yash Kumar Lal, Stony Brook University, New York
Rachel Rudinger, University of Maryland, College Park
Xiang Ren, University of Southern California
Niket Tandon, Allen Institute for AI
Vilém Zouhar, CUNI and UdS

Program Committee

Program Committee

Maarten Sap, Allen Institute for AI
Jack Hessel, Allen Institute for AI
Keisuke Sakaguchi, Allen Institute for AI
Prithviraj Ammanabrolu, Allen Institute for AI
Jeff Da, Allen Institute for AI
Liwei Jiang, University of Washington
Alisa Liu, University of Washington
Rowan Zellers, University of Washington
Lianhui Qin, University of Washington
Ximing Lu, University of Washington
Tuhin Chakrabarty, Columbia University
Emily Allaway, Columbia University
Michi Yasunaga, Stanford University
Xikun Zhang, Stanford University
Deniz Bayazit, EPFL, Switzerland
Silin Gao, EPFL, Switzerland
Shaobo Cui, EPFL, Switzerland
Aman Madaan, Carnegie Mellon University
Khyathi Chandu, Carnegie Mellon University
Yanai Elazar, Bar-Ilan University
Avijit Thawani, University of Southern California
Pei Zhou, University of Southern California
Yu Hou, University of Southern California
Anurag Acharya, Florida International University
Sarah Wiegraffe, Georgia Tech
Neha Srikanth, University of Maryland, College Park
Yue Dong, McGill University
Denis Emelin, University of Edinburgh
Simon Razniewski, Max Planck Institute
Filip Ilievski, USC Information Sciences Institute
Mayank Kejriwal, USC Information Sciences Institute
Manuel Ciosici, USC Information Sciences Institute
Sumit Bhatia, Adobe Research
Faeze Brahman, University of California, Santa Cruz

Invited Speakers

Evelina Fedorenko, Massachusetts Institute of Technology
Tobias Gerstenberg, Stanford University
Greg Durrett, University of Texas, Austin
Prithviraj Ammanabrolu, Allen Institute for AI
Mor Geva, Tel Aviv University, Israel

Table of Contents

Identifying relevant common sense information in knowledge graphs
Guy Aglionby and Simone Tuefel . . . 1

Cloze Evaluation for Deeper Understanding of Commonsense Stories in Indonesian
Fajri Koto, Timothy Baldwin and Jey Han Lau . . . 8

Psycholinguistic Diagnosis of Language Models' Commonsense Reasoning
Yan Cong . . . 17

Bridging the Gap between Recognition-level Pre-training and Commonsensical Vision-language Tasks
Yue Wan, Yueen Ma, Haoxuan You, Zhecan Wang and Shih-Fu Chang . . . 23

Materialized Knowledge Bases from Commonsense Transformers
Tuan-Phong Nguyen and Simon Razniewski . . . 36

Knowledge-Augmented Language Models for Cause-Effect Relation Classification
Pedram Hosseini, David A. Broniatowski and Mona Diab . . . 43

CURIE: An Iterative Querying Approach for Reasoning About Situations
Dheeraj Rajagopal, Aman Madaan, Niket Tandon, Yiming Yang, Shrimai Prabhumoye, Abhilasha Ravichander, Peter Clark and Eduard H Hovy . . . 49

Identifying relevant common sense information in knowledge graphs

Guy Aglionby and **Simone Teufel**
Department of Computer Science and Technology
University of Cambridge
United Kingdom
{guy.aglionby,sht25}@cl.cam.ac.uk

Abstract

Knowledge graphs are often used to store common sense information that is useful for various tasks. However, the extraction of contextually-relevant knowledge is an unsolved problem, and current approaches are relatively simple. Here we introduce a triple selection method based on a ranking model and find that it improves question answering accuracy over existing methods. We additionally investigate methods to ensure that extracted triples form a connected graph. Graph connectivity is important for model interpretability, as paths are frequently used as explanations for the reasoning that connects question and answer.

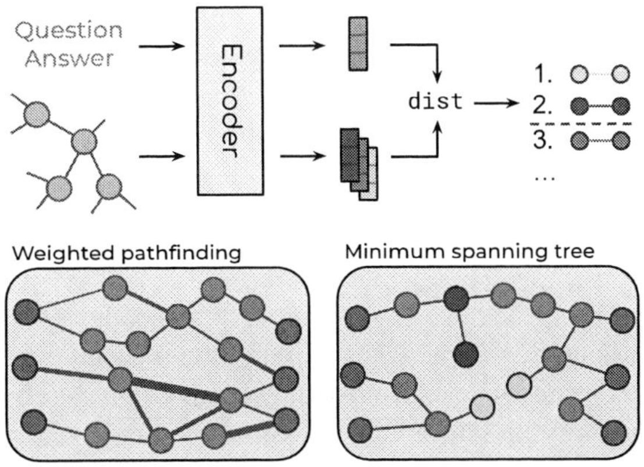

Figure 1: The triple scoring process for a question answering task, and two methods that use the scores to extract relevant subgraphs for a question and candidate answer.

1 Introduction

For models to be able to reason about situations that arise in everyday life, they must have access to contextually appropriate common sense information. This information is commonly stored as a large set of facts from which the model must identify a relevant subset. One approach to structuring these facts is as a knowledge graph. Here, nodes represent high-level concepts, and typed edges represent different kinds of relationship between concepts. In practice, a subset of facts that are thought to be contextually relevant are extracted from the graph, as using all facts in each instance is unnecessary, noisy, and computationally expensive.

Prior work has focused on different ways to encode these facts, including by inputting them into a graph neural network (GNN) or into a transformer (Feng et al., 2020; Yasunaga et al., 2021). However, the question of how to identify useful information has been under-explored, particularly in work that uses GNN encoders. If contextually important information is not retrieved then performance could be dramatically reduced, a potential result of the use of overly simplistic retrieval methods.

In this paper we explore methods to extract high-quality subgraphs containing contextually relevant information.[1] We approach this as a ranking task across triples in a knowledge graph, and propose two methods that use the scores to extract a subgraph. The first is a weighted pathfinding approach which extends prior work (Lin et al., 2019), while the second builds a minimum spanning tree that includes the highest-ranked triples (figure 1). Both approaches ensure that all or most nodes in the subgraph are reachable from each other, which is important for two reasons. First, it means that the GNN can update node embeddings with information from most other nodes, which would not be possible if the graph were disconnected. Second, it allows paths of reasoning to be extracted from the subgraph, which are often used as explanations for model behaviour (Feng et al., 2020; Wang et al., 2020; Yasunaga et al., 2021).

There are also situations when specific concepts need to be included in order for a subgraph to be of high enough quality. For example, in question answering, a full explanation must include one

[1]We call these "relevant subgraphs" or "extracted subgraphs", noting that others use "schema graphs" (Lin et al., 2019).

Proceedings of the First Workshop on Commonsense Representation and Reasoning (CSRR 2021), pages 1 - 7

or more concepts mentioned both in the question and in a candidate answer. This requires robustness towards how concepts identified because the knowledge repository might express the concept in a slightly different lexical form from the question and/or answer. We therefore experiment with a embedding-based method to identify these concepts, and compare it with existing lexical methods.

Our contributions are as follows[2]:

- Apply a ranking model to identify common sense triples that are relevant to some context.
- Identify and thoroughly investigate methods to ensure that the extracted contextually-relevant subgraphs are (almost) connected.
- Compare existing lexical approaches to entity linking to a simple embedding-based method.

2 Background

Many prior approaches to retrieving relevant common sense triples from a knowledge graph start by identifying relevant nodes. Simple lexical overlap between a concept and the context (e.g. question text) is often used for this (Kundu et al., 2019; Khot et al., 2019). However, this entity linking approach is likely to only retrieve simple concepts, as the idiosyncratic phrasing of some node names in knowledge graphs like ConceptNet (Speer et al., 2017) are unlikely to show up in text. Becker et al. (2021) investigate this in detail and propose a series of pre-processing steps that allow lexically-based linking without exact phrase matches. For the same reason, the heuristics used by Lin et al. (2019) for lexical matching are employed by a series of later works (Feng et al., 2020; Yasunaga et al., 2021; Wang et al., 2020). Although lexical matching is a frequent approach with common sense knowledge graphs, in other domains embedding-based approaches are more popular (Gillick et al., 2019). These work by embedding the candidate text and finding the nearest neighbour in the space of entity embeddings.

In question answering, Lin et al. (2019) split these concepts into those identified in the question and in the answer, and find additional concepts for the relevant subgraph by iteratively finding shortest paths between the two sets. This process continues until a maximum number is collected, or the path lengths exceed a threshold. The final subgraph used as input to models is constructed from this set with all valid edges added.

Some approaches score nodes and triples that have been identified. Kundu et al. (2019) score multiple paths for each question and answer and choose the answer with the highest mean path score. Yasunaga et al. (2021) extract a subgraph following Lin et al. (2019), and additionally score each node for relevance to a question using RoBERTa (Liu et al., 2019). Ranking is also common with prose facts, particularly when they are input into transformer-based models that have limits on input size (Wang et al., 2021).

3 Methodology

In this section we introduce our methods for extracting a contextually-relevant subgraph $\mathcal{G}$ for a question answering task. The graph should contain triples that are useful in distinguishing the correct answer from a set of distractors. For each instance, we represent the question text as q and the ith candidate answer as a_i, and the set of concepts extracted from each as C_q and C_{a_i} respectively.

3.1 Triple scoring

We cast the task of identifying relevant triples in the knowledge graph as a ranking problem, where the highest-ranked triples are those most relevant to $q; a_i$. We use an existing model that is trained to rank facts highly if they constitute part of an explanation for why a_i is the correct answer to q (Pan et al., 2021). This was developed for the TextGraphs 2021 shared task on explanation regeneration for science questions (Thayaparan et al., 2021) and achieved the highest performance. Facts that are used in an explanation are likely to be useful when choosing between answers, making the model a natural choice for identifying relevant triples.

The model consists of two parts: a fact retriever and a re-ranker. We follow the training procedure in Pan et al. (2021) and use one model based on RoBERTa-Large (Liu et al., 2019) for each stage. At inference time we use only the re-ranker to score each triple[3] in relation to $q; a_i$. To speed this up we pre-compute embeddings for each $q; a_i$ and each triple.

[2] We make our code and data available at https://github.com/GuyAglionby/kg-common-sense-extraction.

[3] We linearize triples using the templates from https://github.com/commonsense/conceptnet5/wiki/Relations.

3.2 Constructing $\mathcal{G}$

The most straightforward way to construct $\mathcal{G}$ is to use the most relevant triples identified in §3.1 and the grounded nodes $\mathcal{C}_q \cup \mathcal{C}_{a_i}$. To do this, we select a subset of the top e ranked triples according to limits on the total number of edges and nodes that would be added to $\mathcal{G}$. Iterating in rank order, we add the triple (s, r, o) to $\mathcal{G}$ only if adding s and o does not increase the total number of nodes to above n. If $n < 2e$ then some of the top edges will be excluded; this limits the number of nodes in the graph while allowing highly-ranked edges to be present if they share nodes with other edges. We set $n = 50$ and $e = 40$ following initial experiments.

A shortcoming of this method is that the selected triples are not likely to connect with $\mathcal{C}_q$ or $\mathcal{C}_{a_i}$. Indeed, there is no guarantee that the triples are connected to each other. This is problematic in cases where paths in the extracted subgraph are to be used in an explanation (Feng et al., 2020; Yasunaga et al., 2021).

To rectify this we find the minimum spanning tree (MST) that spans all nodes in $\mathcal{G}$, taking into account the edges added in the previous step. This is the Steiner tree problem, which is NP-hard; we apply an approximation algorithm (Wu et al., 1986) to find solutions in a reasonable amount of time. We experiment with two variants: one where edges are uniformly weighted, and another where the triple scores are used as weights.

We further use the triple scores with the pathfinding method used in previous work (Lin et al., 2019), transforming this into a weighted shortest path search. We iteratively find the shortest path between any pair of concepts in $\mathcal{C}_q$ and $\mathcal{C}_{a_i}$, adding nodes on the paths to a set until a maximum size is reached. $\mathcal{G}$ is then formed from these nodes, as well as all valid edges between pairs from this set. We set the maximum number of nodes to be 50.

3.3 Identifying relevant concepts

It is important that $\mathcal{C}_q$ and $\mathcal{C}_{a_i}$ accurately reflect concepts mentioned in q and a, primarily to aid with explanations. A full explanation for a question must include at least one concept from $\mathcal{C}_q$ and from $\mathcal{C}_{a_i}$; if these concepts are nonsensical then the explanation is invalid. Additionally, the pathfinding method for relevant subgraph extraction relies on the quality of this grounding.

We use two methods for entity linking. The first is from prior work, and is based on lexical matching with heuristics (Lin et al., 2019). These include lemmatising words if an exact match is not found, and a method to avoid selecting nodes with lexical overlap. Despite this, lexical methods are not able to identify relevant concepts that have a lexical form that is not likely to be seen in any context; this occurs often with more specific concepts.To account for this, our second method is based on embeddings from `RoBERTa`. We embed each concept, and for each q and a_i find the 10 most similar concepts via Euclidean distance. Embeddings are constructed in each case by mean-pooling across all tokens.

3.4 Evaluation

We evaluate the quality of the extracted subgraphs by comparing accuracy on a question answering task when using them versus using a baseline. These graphs are used as input to two models, MHGRN (Feng et al., 2020) and QA-GNN (Yasunaga et al., 2021), which are both designed for question answering with knowledge graphs. The baseline subgraph is extracted using the unweighted pathfinding method from prior work (Lin et al., 2019); for the fairest comparison we run five baselines which extract subgraphs of different sizes and report the best result from these (see appendix C for full details). We also compare to baseline that uses only `RoBERTa-large` with no additional facts.

We report accuracy on two datasets, OpenbookQA (Mihaylov et al., 2018) and CommonsenseQA (Talmor et al., 2019). OpenbookQA is a collection of science questions, and so is in-domain with respect to the data used to train the fact scorer. CommonsenseQA targets more general common sense; performance here is a reflection on how transferable the fact scorer is to other domains. This dataset has no public test set labels, so we report results on the 'in house' test split defined by Lin et al. (2019). Each model is run three times with different random seeds and the mean accuracy reported. Model hyperparameters are reported in appendix A.

Our base knowledge graph is ConceptNet (Speer et al., 2017). Following previous work (Lin et al., 2019), we merge similar relations and add reverse relations to the extracted graph.

Grounding	Subgraph type	MHGRN	QA-GNN
LM Only		62.07	
Lexical	*Baseline*	**67.73**	**67.07**
	Only top rated	62.73	64.47
Lexical	MST	63.07	64.27
	Weighted MST	64.87	60.73
	Weighted path	64.20	65.27
Embedding	MST	65.47	66.33
	Weighted MST	64.73	64.60
	Weighted path	64.07	65.73

Table 1: Accuracy on **OpenbookQA** with different subgraph extraction methods.

Grounding	Subgraph type	MHGRN	QA-GNN
LM Only		69.53	
Lexical	*Baseline*	69.48	70.32
	Only top rated	69.76	69.92
Lexical	MST	69.86*	69.35
	Weighted MST	69.19	**70.64***
	Weighted path	69.86*	68.87
Embedding	MST	69.60	70.10
	Weighted MST	**69.97***	69.86
	Weighted path	69.27	70.08

Table 2: Accuracy on **CommonsenseQA** with different subgraph extraction methods.[5]

4 Results

Our results on OpenbookQA are presented in table 1 and CommonsenseQA in table 2. On CommonsenseQA, our best method significantly[4] outperforms the baseline method. This suggests that, in this case, the ranker is able to identify facts which are relevant to the question, and that the models are subsequently able to successfully use them.

The tuned baseline for OpenbookQA beats the proposed methods in all cases, although there is reasonable variation in accuracy between the baselines of different sizes (see table 6). However, in all but two cases the methods for ensuring graph connectivity outperform the method that only uses the highest-ranked triples.

5 Analysis

We observe that, in the majority of cases, using methods to increase connectivity within the extracted subgraph improves performance over simply including the top rated facts. The minimum spanning tree (MST) approach has the advantage of including these facts, unlike the weighted path method which may not. However, to ensure that the graph is connected the MST approach may have to include nodes and edges that are less relevant to the context. One might expect a weighted approach to counterbalance this, however this also results in a larger subgraph being constructed which may be detrimental (see appendix B). Indeed, with lexical grounding the weighted approach adds an average of 37 nodes and 83 edges to the extracted subgraph, compared with 26 nodes and 71 edges in the unweighted case.

The weighted pathfinding approach has the advantage of avoiding edges which are not relevant to the query. Additionally, the subgraph is extracted in way that is closer to $\mathcal{C}_q$ and $\mathcal{C}_{a_i}$ than the MST approach, which considers these nodes only after selecting the top-ranked triples. As a result, the question and answer nodes are connected in a larger variety of ways, which may help increase performance.

For OpenbookQA, the increase in score between lexical and embedding-based entity linking with an unweighted MST suggests that the concepts identified by the latter method are particularly useful. The same magnitude of increase is not seen in CommonsenseQA. One possible reason for this is that CommonsenseQA was constructed directly using ConceptNet, which may increase the relevance of concepts obtained with lexical methods.

Similarly to with lexical grounding, the weighted MST with embedding grounding adds more nodes and edges on average (153 nodes, 217 edges) than the unweighted one (112 nodes, 172 edges). In both cases, the resulting subgraph is substantially larger than the equivalent ones built from lexically-linked entities. This is likely due to the kinds of nodes identified by entity linking – we observe that concepts identified by the embedding-based method are more specific, and so are less connected within the overall graph. Conversely, concepts that are identified lexically are likely to be simpler and more general, and so better connected within the graph, meaning fewer additional nodes and edges are required to build the MST.

[4]We use the Almost Stochastic Dominance test (Dror et al., 2019) and only claim a significant difference if $\epsilon \leq 0.05$.

[5]* denotes significantly better than baseline subgraph at $p < 0.001$.

6 Conclusion

We present a method for extracting relevant information from a common sense knowledge graph, casting it as a ranking problem. We show that scores obtained from a ranking model can be used to select triples containing useful information for a question answering task, improving performance over a commonly-used approach.

As it is undesirable for extracted subgraphs to have low connectivity, particularly when using paths within them for model interpretation, we use an algorithm for calculating minimum spanning trees over a supplied set of nodes and edges to ensure the graph is connected. We find that this helps performance; in particular, the models with highest accuracy on CommonsenseQA use a weighted version of this. We additionally find that using an entity linking approach that uses embeddings rather than lexical matching improves performance in some cases. We distribute the contextually-relevant subgraphs to facilitate future work; these drop in to existing models with no further processing required.

Future work might investigate the influence of the fact ranker, as our results suggest that it can transfer from the science to general common sense domain successfully. Further training of the ranker using higher-quality negative samples from e-QASC (Jhamtani and Clark, 2020) may yield better performance, as noted by Pan et al. (2021).

References

Maria Becker, Katharina Korfhage, and Anette Frank. 2021. COCO-EX: A tool for linking concepts from texts to ConceptNet. In *Proceedings of the 16th Conference of the European Chapter of the Association for Computational Linguistics: System Demonstrations*, pages 119–126, Online. Association for Computational Linguistics.

Rotem Dror, Segev Shlomov, and Roi Reichart. 2019. Deep dominance - how to properly compare deep neural models. In *Proceedings of the 57th Annual Meeting of the Association for Computational Linguistics*, pages 2773–2785, Florence, Italy. Association for Computational Linguistics.

Yanlin Feng, Xinyue Chen, Bill Yuchen Lin, Peifeng Wang, Jun Yan, and Xiang Ren. 2020. Scalable multi-hop relational reasoning for knowledge-aware question answering. In *Proceedings of the 2020 Conference on Empirical Methods in Natural Language Processing (EMNLP)*, pages 1295–1309, Online. Association for Computational Linguistics.

Daniel Gillick, Sayali Kulkarni, Larry Lansing, Alessandro Presta, Jason Baldridge, Eugene Ie, and Diego Garcia-Olano. 2019. Learning dense representations for entity retrieval. In *Proceedings of the 23rd Conference on Computational Natural Language Learning (CoNLL)*, pages 528–537, Hong Kong, China. Association for Computational Linguistics.

Harsh Jhamtani and Peter Clark. 2020. Learning to Explain: Datasets and Models for Identifying Valid Reasoning Chains in Multihop Question-Answering. In *Proceedings of the 2020 Conference on Empirical Methods in Natural Language Processing (EMNLP)*, pages 137–150, Online. Association for Computational Linguistics.

Tushar Khot, Ashish Sabharwal, and Peter Clark. 2019. What's missing: A knowledge gap guided approach for multi-hop question answering. In *Proceedings of the 2019 Conference on Empirical Methods in Natural Language Processing and the 9th International Joint Conference on Natural Language Processing (EMNLP-IJCNLP)*, pages 2814–2828, Hong Kong, China. Association for Computational Linguistics.

Souvik Kundu, Tushar Khot, Ashish Sabharwal, and Peter Clark. 2019. Exploiting explicit paths for multi-hop reading comprehension. In *Proceedings of the 57th Annual Meeting of the Association for Computational Linguistics*, pages 2737–2747, Florence, Italy. Association for Computational Linguistics.

Bill Yuchen Lin, Xinyue Chen, Jamin Chen, and Xiang Ren. 2019. KagNet: Knowledge-aware graph networks for commonsense reasoning. In *Proceedings of the 2019 Conference on Empirical Methods in Natural Language Processing and the 9th International Joint Conference on Natural Language Processing (EMNLP-IJCNLP)*, pages 2829–2839, Hong Kong, China. Association for Computational Linguistics.

Liyuan Liu, Haoming Jiang, Pengcheng He, Weizhu Chen, Xiaodong Liu, Jianfeng Gao, and Jiawei Han. 2021. On the Variance of the Adaptive Learning Rate and Beyond. *arXiv:1908.03265 [cs, stat]*.

Yinhan Liu, Myle Ott, Naman Goyal, Jingfei Du, Mandar Joshi, Danqi Chen, Omer Levy, Mike Lewis, Luke Zettlemoyer, and Veselin Stoyanov. 2019. RoBERTa: A Robustly Optimized BERT Pretraining Approach. *arXiv:1907.11692*.

Todor Mihaylov, Peter Clark, Tushar Khot, and Ashish Sabharwal. 2018. Can a suit of armor conduct electricity? a new dataset for open book question answering. In *Proceedings of the 2018 Conference on Empirical Methods in Natural Language Processing*, pages 2381–2391, Brussels, Belgium. Association for Computational Linguistics.

Chunguang Pan, Bingyan Song, and Zhipeng Luo. 2021. DeepBlueAI at TextGraphs 2021 shared task: Treating multi-hop inference explanation regeneration as a ranking problem. In *Proceedings of the Fifteenth Workshop on Graph-Based Methods for Natural Language Processing (TextGraphs-15)*, pages 166–170,

Mexico City, Mexico. Association for Computational Linguistics.

Robyn Speer, Joshua Chin, and Catherine Havasi. 2017. ConceptNet 5.5: An Open Multilingual Graph of General Knowledge. In *Thirty-First AAAI Conference on Artificial Intelligence*.

Alon Talmor, Jonathan Herzig, Nicholas Lourie, and Jonathan Berant. 2019. CommonsenseQA: A question answering challenge targeting commonsense knowledge. In *Proceedings of the 2019 Conference of the North American Chapter of the Association for Computational Linguistics: Human Language Technologies, Volume 1 (Long and Short Papers)*, pages 4149–4158, Minneapolis, Minnesota. Association for Computational Linguistics.

Mokanarangan Thayaparan, Marco Valentino, Peter Jansen, and Dmitry Ustalov. 2021. TextGraphs 2021 shared task on multi-hop inference for explanation regeneration. In *Proceedings of the Fifteenth Workshop on Graph-Based Methods for Natural Language Processing (TextGraphs-15)*, pages 156–165, Mexico City, Mexico. Association for Computational Linguistics.

Han Wang, Yang Liu, Chenguang Zhu, Linjun Shou, Ming Gong, Yichong Xu, and Michael Zeng. 2021. Retrieval enhanced model for commonsense generation. In *Findings of the Association for Computational Linguistics: ACL-IJCNLP 2021*, pages 3056–3062, Online. Association for Computational Linguistics.

Peifeng Wang, Nanyun Peng, Filip Ilievski, Pedro Szekely, and Xiang Ren. 2020. Connecting the dots: A knowledgeable path generator for commonsense question answering. In *Findings of the Association for Computational Linguistics: EMNLP 2020*, pages 4129–4140, Online. Association for Computational Linguistics.

Ying Fung Wu, Peter Widmayer, and Chak Kuen Wong. 1986. A faster approximation algorithm for the steiner problem in graphs. *Acta Informatica*, 23(2):223–229.

Michihiro Yasunaga, Hongyu Ren, Antoine Bosselut, Percy Liang, and Jure Leskovec. 2021. QA-GNN: Reasoning with language models and knowledge graphs for question answering. In *Proceedings of the 2021 Conference of the North American Chapter of the Association for Computational Linguistics: Human Language Technologies*, pages 535–546, Online. Association for Computational Linguistics.

A Hyperparameters

We use the same hyperparameters for MHGRN and QA-GNN as used in the papers which respectively introduced them (Feng et al., 2020; Yasunaga et al., 2021). We optimise both models using RAdam (Liu et al., 2021) and a learning rate of $1e-3$ for the text encoder and $1e-5$ for the graph encoder. A maximum of 128 tokens are input to the text encoder, which is initialised as `RoBERTa-large`. A L2 weight decay of 0.01 is used.

For MHGRN, batch size is 32 and the text encoder is frozen for the first 3 epochs. A 1-layer 100-dimensional GNN is used with 3-hop message passing at each layer.

For QA-GNN, batch size is 128 and the text encoder is frozen for the first 4 epochs. A 5-layer 200-dimensional GNN is used.

In all cases, the GNN is initialised with node embeddings derived from BERT, which are made available by Feng et al. (2020).

B Extracted subgraph size

For each type of extracted subgraph, we report the mean and standard deviation of the number of edges in table 3 and number of nodes in table 4. We report results for the baselines in table 5.

Grounding	Subgraph type	OBQA	CSQA
Lexical	Only top rated	33±6	28±5
	MST	104±28	110±29
	Weighted MST	117±30	123±32
	Weighted path	216±50	232±54
Embedding	MST	202±50	201±46
	Weighted MST	245±64	250±56
	Weighted path	168±43	177±47

Table 3: Average number of edges in extracted subgraphs for OpenbookQA and CommonsenseQA.

Grounding	Subgraph type	OBQA	CSQA
Lexical	Only top rated	49±2	50
	MST	78±22	77±21
	Weighted MST	89±23	89±23
	Weighted path	53±5	54±4
Embedding	MST	167±41	162±35
	Weighted MST	207±53	206±45
	Weighted path	59±3	58±2

Table 4: Average number of nodes in extracted subgraphs for OpenbookQA and CommonsenseQA.

Nodes/edges	Model	OBQA	CSQA
Nodes	MHGRN	50±10	36±7
	QA-GNN	63±12	63±12
Edges	MHGRN	128±23	64±13
	QA-GNN	190±33	188±36

Table 5: Average number of nodes and edges in baseline subgraphs for OpenbookQA and CommonsenseQA.

Target edge count	MHGRN	QA-GNN
50	65.27	65.20
100	**67.73**	65.87
150	63.53	**67.07**
200	65.27	66.53
250	64.40	64.20

Table 6: Accuracy on **OpenbookQA** when using the baseline subgraph extraction method with five different target edge counts.

Target edge count	MHGRN	QA-GNN
50	**69.48**	70.08
100	68.60	69.83
150	69.11	**70.32**
200	68.95	69.54
250	69.46	69.33

Table 7: Accuracy on **CommonsenseQA** when using the baseline subgraph extraction method with five different target edge counts.

C Baseline models

Subgraph size is a confounding factor when comparing performance between our extraction methods and the baseline (Lin et al., 2019). To control for this, we extract baseline subgraphs of five different sizes by expanding them until they reach a certain number of edges. In tables 1 and 2 we report the only highest scoring baseline; full baseline results are presented in tables 6 and 7.

Cloze Evaluation for Deeper Understanding of Commonsense Stories in Indonesian

Fajri Koto[1] **Timothy Baldwin**[1,2] **Jey Han Lau**[1]
[1]The University of Melbourne
[2]MBZUAI
ffajri@student.unimelb.edu.au, tb@ldwin.net, jeyhan.lau@gmail.com

Abstract

Story comprehension that involves complex causal and temporal relations is a critical task in NLP, but previous studies have focused predominantly on English, leaving open the question of how the findings generalize to other languages, such as Indonesian. In this paper, we follow the Story Cloze Test framework of Mostafazadeh et al. (2016) in evaluating story understanding in Indonesian, by constructing a four-sentence story with one correct ending and one incorrect ending. To investigate commonsense knowledge acquisition in language models, we experimented with: (1) a classification task to predict the correct ending; and (2) a generation task to complete the story with a single sentence. We investigate these tasks in two settings: (i) monolingual training and (ii) zero-shot cross-lingual transfer between Indonesian and English.

1 Introduction

Commonsense reasoning is a key component of natural language understanding (NLU), which previous work (Charniak, 1972; Mueller, 2004; Mostafazadeh et al., 2016; Chen et al., 2019) has attempted to model through tasks such as story comprehension. While humans can easily comprehend temporal and causal relations to understand a story narrative, machines tend to struggle due to implicit information and story premises. Often, *world knowledge* such as social conventions, the laws of nature, and common logic are required to connect the premises to draw appropriate conclusions or closure (Shoham, 1990; Ponti et al., 2020).

Mostafazadeh et al. (2016) and Sharma et al. (2018) introduced the *Story Cloze Test* framework to empirically evaluate commonsense reasoning, based on English short stories about daily-life events. The task is to choose the correct ending of a four-sentence story based on a two-way multiple choice. Mostafazadeh et al. (2016) published 3,700 data pairs, and the dataset has been used to model commonsense reasoning (Schwartz et al., 2017; Liu et al., 2018; Sap et al., 2019; Chen et al., 2019; Li et al., 2019) and perform discourse probing of pretrained language models (Koto et al., 2021).

There is a lack of research modeling story comprehension in languages beyond English. Ponti et al. (2020) argued that current progress over English may not generalize to other languages because of its Anglocentric bias both linguistically, and also in terms of cultural and social conventions (Thomas, 1983). Motivated by this, we explore commonsense reasoning in Indonesian by constructing a dataset based on the framework of Mostafazadeh et al. (2016).

XCOPA (Ponti et al., 2020) is perhaps the most closely-related work to ours, wherein 600 instances of the COPA dataset (Roemmele et al., 2011) were manually translated into 11 languages, including Indonesian. COPA is an open-domain commonsense causal reasoning task that consists of two-sentence pairs, and does not include complex narrative comprehension. Moreover, the translation approach also has its own limitations, in entrenching Anglocentric social contexts in other languages.

To summarize, we introduce the first Story Cloze Test in Indonesian, and perform preliminary studies based on: (1) a classification task to predict the correct ending (Li et al., 2019); and (2) a single-sentence generation task to complete the story (Guan et al., 2019; Huang et al., 2021). We perform these two tasks in two settings: (1) monolingual training, and (2) zero-shot cross-lingual transfer, between Indonesian and English. Our data and code are available at https://github.com/fajri91/IndoCloze.

2 Dataset Construction

Following Mostafazadeh et al. (2016), we construct an Indonesian Story Cloze Test dataset. Each instance consists of a four-sentence premise, and two candidates for the fifth sentence: an appropriate

Proceedings of the First Workshop on Commonsense Representation and Reasoning (CSRR 2021), pages 8 - 16
May 27, 2022

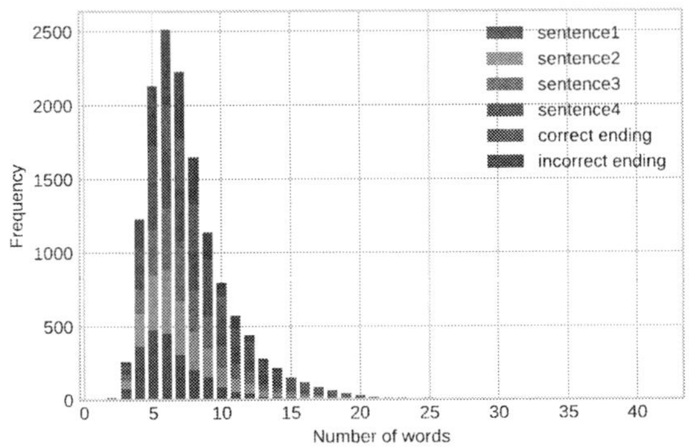

Figure 1: Number of words in each sentence position.

Person (#unique: 1962)	**Location** (#unique: 114)	**Organization** (#unique: 166)
Rio, Acha, Reno, Mamat, Hana, Gina, Juju, Tarra, Maria, Elisa	Indonesia, Jakarta, Bandung, Kenya, Bali, Jogja, Surabaya, Korea, Monas	SD Harapan, KAI, SMA Harapan, SMA Angkasa, Bobo, Bimbel, SMP Harapan

Table 1: Examples of `PERSON`, `LOCATION`, and `ORGANIZATION` (sampled from top-20 predictions).

and inappropriate ending. Similar to Mostafazadeh et al. (2016) and Sharma et al. (2018), our corpus consists of daily-life events, but in Indonesian contexts (e.g. locations, places, names, food, culture).

Data creation. We hired seven Indonesian university students to each write 500 short stories over a period of one month. As part of the recruitment, candidates were provided with story requirements and several examples,[1] and asked to write a 5-sentence story, as well as an inappropriate fifth sentence. From ten applicants, we hired the seven best candidates based on their submitted stories. After one month, four workers completed the job and were paid Rp 750,000.[2] The three who did not complete the task were paid a prorated salary, based on the number of completed stories. This resulted in a dataset of 2,335 stories (see Table 2 for examples).

Quality control. We additionally assessed the dataset by employing two Indonesian university students that were not involved in the data construction.[3] Based on 100 random samples, we asked each worker to choose the correct fifth sentence for a given four-sentence premise, and found that both workers achieved 99% accuracy.[4]

Data statistics. Our corpus contains 14,010 sentences and 106,479 words. In Figure 1, we observe that word counts in each sentence position are somewhat similar, with a median sentence length of 5–10 words.

We used an IndoBERT model (Koto et al., 2020) to train POS and NER models, based on the datasets of Dinakaramani et al. (2014) and Gultom and Wibowo (2017), resp., and used them to predict `VERB`, `PERSON`, `LOCATION`, and `ORGANIZATION` tags.[5] First, we found that the dataset contains 21,447 `VERB` tokens (3,723 unique tokens), with the top-3 most frequent verbs having a frequency of 2% (see Figure 2 in Appendix). We also observe that `PERSON`, `LOCATION`, and `ORGANIZATION` NEs are mostly local Indonesian expressions, with common `PERSON` names being *Reno* and *Mamat*, and organization names being *KAI* and *Bobo*, as captured in Table 1. Additionally, we found that the top-5 most frequent bigrams and trigrams have a frequency of less than 0.3%, demonstrating the lexical diversity of our stories, even though the dataset was created by a small number of workers (Table 3).

3 Experimental Setup

Similar to Bhagavatula et al. (2020) experiments in English commonsense reasoning, we conducted two tasks: (1) a classification task to predict the correct ending; and (2) a single-sentence generation task to complete the story. We perform these two tasks in two settings: (1) monolingual training, and (2) zero-shot cross-lingual transfer, between Indonesian and English. The data split is presented in Table 4.

3.1 Classification

Following Mostafazadeh et al. (2016), we evaluate the classification task based on accuracy, defined as $\frac{\#correct}{\#testcases}$. Models are tuned based on the development set, and results are averaged over three runs. We experiment with the following four models.

n**-gram overlap**: We select candidate with the highest ROUGE-1 (F1; Lin (2004)), computed between the premise and ending.

`fastText`-based similarity: We pick the candidate with the highest cosine similarity, computed

[1] See Appendix for more details.

[2] The monthly minimum wage in Indonesia is around Rp 4,000,000, and the workload to write 500 short stories equates to roughly 5-days of full-time work.

[3] We paid Rp 150,000 to each.

[4] The two candidate fifth sentences (the correct and incorrect endings) are shuffled for each story.

[5] The POS and NER models have accuracies of 96.8% and 90.1%, respectively.

	Indonesian	English
Context	*Sepulang sekolah, Rani dan Rina mengunjungi toko komik. Komik kesukaan mereka terbit hari ini. Masing-masing membayar sepuluh ribu rupiah. Setelah membayar, mereka berdua pulang ke rumah*	After school, Rani and Rina visit a comic shop. Their favorite comic will be published today. Each of them paid ten thousand rupiah. After paying, the two of them went home.
Right ending	*Mereka membaca komik itu bersama-sama di rumah.*	They read the comic together at home.
Wrong ending	*Komik itu mereka robek jadi dua bagian.*	They tore the comic into two parts.
Context	*Hari ini langit sangat mendung. Gemuruh sudah terdengar sejak pagi. Diprediksi hujan akan segera turun. Aku bergegas berangkat kerja karena takut kehujanan.*	Today the sky is very cloudy. There has been thunder since morning. It is predicted that rain will fall soon. I rush to work to avoid the rain.
Right ending	*Aku membawa jas hujan.*	I take a raincoat.
Wrong ending	*Sebelum berangkat, aku menjemur pakaian di halaman rumah*	Before leaving, I hang my washing outdoors.
Context	*Boni punya 5 balon. Balon ini dibelikan oleh ayah di Jalan Margonda. Semua balon Boni berwarna berbeda. 2 balon berwarna merah dan biru.*	Boni has 5 balloons. These balloons were bought by his father at Jalan Margonda. All Boni's balloons are different colours. Two of the balloons are red and blue.
Right ending	*Yang lain berwarna putih, hitam, dan kuning*	The others are white, black and yellow.
Wrong ending	*Sedangkan ketiga lainnya berwarna merah muda.*	While the other three are pink.

Table 2: Three example Story Cloze Test instances, with an English translation for illustrative purposes.

Bigram (#unique: 59,256)	**Freq (%)**
pergi ke (go to)	0.30
tidak bisa (can not)	0.29
hari ini (today)	0.27
teman temannya (his/her friends)	0.25
tidak pernah (never)	0.25
Trigram (#unique: 72,443)	**Freq (%)**
oleh karena itu (therefore/thus)	0.04
pulang ke rumah (go home)	0.04
dengan teman temannya (with his/her friends)	0.03
maka dari itu (therefore/thus)	0.03
dan teman temannya (and his/her friends)	0.03

Table 3: Top-5 bigrams and trigrams.

Task	EN	ID (ours)
Classification	1,683 / 188 / 1,871	1,000 / 200 / 1,135
Generation	45,496 / 1,871 / 1,871	1,000 / 200 / 1,135

Table 4: Data distribution of train/development/test set. The English dataset is from Mostafazadeh et al. (2016).

between the premise and ending based on 300d Indonesian `fastText` (Bojanowski et al., 2017).

Hierarchical BiLSTM: We use a two-level 200d BiLSTM, using the first to encode a single sentence with 300d `fastText` as input. We perform average pooling to obtain a sentence representation, and apply the second BiLSTM across all sentences. We concatenate the last hidden state of the two LSTMs, and perform binary classification using a sigmoid function (see Appendix for hyper-parameters).

Pretrained Language Models: We fine-tune MBERT (Devlin et al., 2019) and INDOBERT (Koto et al., 2020) by concatenating the premise and ending sentence, and use `[CLS]` for classification (see Appendix for hyper-parameters).[6]

For classification, we first evaluate the difficulty of our dataset by predicting the fifth sentence based on a different combination of premises as context. For zero-shot cross-lingual transfer, we use the English corpus of Mostafazadeh et al. (2016), and also use translations from Google Translate.[7]

3.2 Generation

We use the four-sentence premise as input, and train MBART (Liu et al., 2020) to generate the fifth sentence for both English and Indonesian. For English, we use the 45K stories of Mostafazadeh et al. (2016) as the training set (see Table 4) and perform zero-shot cross-lingual transfer in both language directions (see Appendix for hyper-parameters).

For automatic evaluation we use ROUGE-L (Lin, 2004), BLEU-4 (Papineni et al., 2002), METEOR (Lavie and Agarwal, 2007), and BERTScore (Zhang et al., 2020). For Indonesian, we also conducted manual evaluation using 4 models $\times$ 50 randomly-sampled test instances, including gold sentences and predicted sentences, trained on the EN, ID, and EN+ID datasets. We asked two native speakers to read the premise and then examine whether the fifth sentence is coherent Indonesian text, does not contain repetition, follows commonsense, contains natural or unnatural code-switching

[6] We use the Huggingface Pytorch framework for fine-tuning (Wolf et al., 2019).

[7] https://translate.google.com/; accessed on April 2021.

Context	n-gram	fastText	LSTM	mBERT	IndoBERT
None	—	—	68.4 ± 1.5	75.7 ± 0.9	76.1 ± 3.4
s_4	40.2	58.9	68.8 ± 1.9	77.1 ± 1.4	78.1 ± 0.3
$s_3 \rightarrow s_4$	49.5	62.3	69.5 ± 0.5	77.3 ± 1.5	76.0 ± 7.8
$s_2 \rightarrow s_4$	**52.9**	62.5	68.6 ± 0.9	77.8 ± 0.9	75.4 ± 0.9
$s_1 \rightarrow s_4$	52.8	**62.6**	**70.0 ± 2.1**	**78.2 ± 1.4**	**81.0 ± 2.1**

Table 5: Test classification accuracy (%) based on different contexts (s_i indicates i-th sentence). Human accuracy is 99 (from 100 samples).

Train	Test (EN)	Test (ID)
EN	81.9 ± 0.5	71.3 ± 2.3
ID	68.1 ± 1.9	**78.2 ± 1.4**
EN+ID	81.7 ± 1.0	76.8 ± 1.1
EN′	69.2 ± 1.5	75.6 ± 0.6
ID′	78.0 ± 0.9	69.6 ± 0.4
EN+EN′	**82.9 ± 0.3**	75.7 ± 1.5
ID+ID′	78.6 ± 0.6	76.2 ± 0.6

Table 6: Test classification accuracy for English (EN) and Indonesian (ID) using mBERT. EN′ and ID′ indicate English and Indonesian translations, respectively, from Google Translate.

Train	Test (EN)				Test (ID)			
	R-L	B	M	BS	R-L	B	M	BS
EN	**20.4**	**6.9**	**9.2**	**75.2**	**19.2**	**6.6**	**8.2**	73.8
ID	8.5	4.5	4.0	70.3	17.6	6.2	7.6	74.4
EN+ID	13.6	5.2	6.3	72.4	18.6	6.4	8.0	**74.7**

Table 7: Fifth-sentence generation using mBART over the test set (R-L, B, M, and BS indicate ROUGE-L, BLEU-4, METEOR, and BERTScore, respectively).

Train	A↑	B↑	C↑	D↑
Gold	94	99	99	81
EN	72	**66**	58	**31**
ID	**92**	52	90	25
EN+ID	**92**	47	**97**	**31**

Table 8: Manual evaluation of the generation task for 50 randomly Indonesian samples, in terms of whether the fifth-sentence: **A**: does not contain repetition; **B**: follows commonsense; **C**: is fluent Indonesian; **D**: has good narrative flow. The presented scores are aggregated across two annotators (in %). The Kappa scores for each category range between 0.4–0.8 (see Appendix).

(in the case there is code-switching), and the overall story has good narrative flow.[8]

4 Results and Analysis

Classification. In Table 5, we find that a 1-sentence premise (s_4) is inadequate to comprehend the narrative of the story. We also observe that the n-gram method performs at near-random (52.9%), while fastText also struggles at 62.6% accuracy. The hierarchical BiLSTM and mBERT perform substantially better, at 70% and 78.2%, respectively.

Overall, the best performance is achieved by IndoBERT when using all sentences ($s_1 \rightarrow s_4$) as context, outperforming mBERT with 81% accuracy. Compared to the English Story Cloze Test, our corpus is arguably harder, as Li et al. (2019) reported BERT accuracies of 78% and 88.1% in the English corpus when using None and $s_1 \rightarrow s_4$ as the premise. We acknowledge that there is a spurious correlation of sentence-5 candidates with the commonsense labels, indicated by IndoBERT accuracy of 76.1% when having context of None. This phenomenon is worse in the English dataset (Mostafazadeh et al., 2016) where the BERT accuracy of using context of None is 88.1% (Li et al., 2019).

In Table 6, we use mBERT to examine commonsense reasoning crosslingually between English (EN) and Indonesian (ID). To simplify, we use L1→L2 to denote training in language L1 and testing in L2. First, we observe that combining EN and ID training worsens commonsense reasoning in both English and Indonesian. Applying zero-shot learning (i.e. EN→ID and ID→EN) achieves mixed results, and ID→EN has worse cross-lingual transfer than EN→ID in terms of performance gap over monolingual training. We argue this is because: (1) English is the dominant language in mBERT training, and (2) our ID corpus contains

[8]Each worker was paid Rp 250,000.

contexts that are less universal (e.g. *nasi padang*[9] vs. *hamburger*).

To further observe whether the transferability is affected by factors beyond language, we translate the training data with Google Translate. In Table 6, EN′ denotes the English translation of the Indonesian training set, and ID′ vice versa. Surprisingly, we found that ID′ →ID has worse performance than EN→ID, while EN′ →EN improves slightly over ID→EN. This suggests that translating the training set to the test language is ineffective, and actually hurts performance for the ID test set. To further explore this effect, we asked two expert workers to evaluate 100 random sentences in the Google Translate output for EN–ID and ID–EN, and found quality in both translation directions to be high, with very little difference in terms of adequacy and fluency (4.5–4.6 out of 5).[10]

Generation. In Table 7, we observe that training using EN achieves the best performance across the automatic metrics on both the EN and ID test sets, with the one exception of BERTScore for EN+ID→ID.[11] However, in the manual evaluation of Indonesian (Table 8), we observe a different trend, in that training using the EN data tends to generate repetitive fifth sentences. Based on the manual evaluation, the best results are using ID and EN+ID as the training data, where the models do not suffer from repetition, generate fluent Indonesian, with similar acceptability in terms of commonsense reasoning.

Although zero-shot cross-lingual transfer of EN→ID suffers from repetition, we notice that MBART is capable of generating plausibly code-mixed sentences made up of Indonesian and English (Gardner-Chloros et al., 2009). Based on our manual evaluation on the same 50 Indonesian test set, we found that 41% of generated fifth sentences contain code-mixing, of which 75% are naturalistic (see Table 9 for examples).

5 Conclusion

In this paper, we introduced the first Indonesian story cloze dataset, and performed preliminary analysis in classification and generation settings in two scenarios: monolingual training and zero-shot cross-lingual transfer between Indonesian and English. From both experiments, we found that the cross-lingual transfer of commonsense from English to Indonesian does not perform well, motivating the construction of commonsense reasoning resources in different languages.

[9]Indonesian cuisine.

[10]Please see Appendix for the adequacy and fluency scores (including Pearson correlations) of each translation system.

[11]EN+ID means that we train the model in a pipeline, using EN first, then ID.

Natural code-mixing sentence
Now Armend memiliki printer di rumahnya (Now Armend has a printer in his house)
The only time Livia keluar kamar, adalah ketika ia sedang tidur The only time Livia left the room is when she sleeps

Unnatural code-mixing sentence
He Hendrik ditangkap oleh Polda (He Hendrik is arrested by the local police)
Shearing her teeth ketika diminta untuk menyanyi paling keras! (Shearing her teeth when she is asked to sing loudly!)

Table 9: Example of code-mixing sentence, generated by MBART when trained on the EN dataset. Red font denotes English words.

6 Ethical Considerations

We paid our expert workers fairly, based on the monthly minimum wage in Indonesia. All workers were made aware that the submitted stories would be distributed, and used for research purposes. No sensitive information about the workers will be released.

Acknowledgments

We are grateful to the anonymous reviewers for their helpful feedback and suggestions. The first author is supported by the Australia Awards Scholarship (AAS), funded by the Department of Foreign Affairs and Trade (DFAT), Australia.

References

Chandra Bhagavatula, Ronan Le Bras, Chaitanya Malaviya, Keisuke Sakaguchi, Ari Holtzman, Hannah Rashkin, Doug Downey, Wen-tau Yih, and Yejin Choi. 2020. Abductive commonsense reasoning. In *ICLR*.

Piotr Bojanowski, Edouard Grave, Armand Joulin, and Tomas Mikolov. 2017. Enriching word vectors with subword information. *Transactions of the Association for Computational Linguistics*, 5:135–146.

Eugene Charniak. 1972. *Toward a model of children's story comprehension.* Ph.D. thesis, Massachusetts Institute of Technology.

Jiaao Chen, Jianshu Chen, and Zhou Yu. 2019. Incorporating structured commonsense knowledge in story completion. In *Proceedings of the AAAI Conference on Artificial Intelligence*, pages 6244–6251.

Jacob Devlin, Ming-Wei Chang, Kenton Lee, and Kristina Toutanova. 2019. BERT: Pre-training of deep bidirectional transformers for language understanding. In *Proceedings of the 2019 Conference of the North American Chapter of the Association for Computational Linguistics: Human Language Technologies, Volume 1 (Long and Short Papers)*, pages 4171–4186, Minneapolis, Minnesota. Association for Computational Linguistics.

Arawinda Dinakaramani, Fam Rashel, Andry Luthfi, and Ruli Manurung. 2014. Designing an Indonesian part of speech tagset and manually tagged Indonesian corpus. In *2014 International Conference on Asian Language Processing (IALP)*, pages 66–69. IEEE.

Penelope Gardner-Chloros et al. 2009. *Code-switching*. Cambridge university press.

Jian Guan, Yansen Wang, and Minlie Huang. 2019. Story ending generation with incremental encoding and commonsense knowledge. In *AAAI*.

Yohanes Gultom and Wahyu Catur Wibowo. 2017. Automatic open domain information extraction from Indonesian text. In *2017 International Workshop on Big Data and Information Security (IWBIS)*, pages 23–30.

Qingbao Huang, Linzhang Mo, Pijian Li, Yi Cai, Qingguang Liu, Jielong Wei, Qing Li, and Ho fung Leung. 2021. Story ending generation with multi-level graph convolutional networks over dependency trees. In *AAAI*.

Philipp Koehn and Christof Monz. 2006. Manual and automatic evaluation of machine translation between European languages. In *Proceedings on the Workshop on Statistical Machine Translation*, pages 102–121, New York City. Association for Computational Linguistics.

Fajri Koto, Jey Han Lau, and Timothy Baldwin. 2021. Discourse probing of pretrained language models. In *Proceedings of the 2021 Conference of the North American Chapter of the Association for Computational Linguistics: Human Language Technologies*, pages 3849–3864, Online. Association for Computational Linguistics.

Fajri Koto, Afshin Rahimi, Jey Han Lau, and Timothy Baldwin. 2020. IndoLEM and IndoBERT: A benchmark dataset and pre-trained language model for Indonesian NLP. In *Proceedings of the 28th International Conference on Computational Linguistics*, pages 757–770, Barcelona, Spain (Online). International Committee on Computational Linguistics.

Alon Lavie and Abhaya Agarwal. 2007. METEOR: An automatic metric for MT evaluation with high levels of correlation with human judgments. In *Proceedings of the Second Workshop on Statistical Machine Translation*, pages 228–231, Prague, Czech Republic. Association for Computational Linguistics.

Zhongyang Li, Xiao Ding, and Ting Liu. 2019. Story ending prediction by transferable bert. In *Proceedings of the Twenty-Eighth International Joint Conference on Artificial Intelligence*, pages 1800–1806.

Chin-Yew Lin. 2004. ROUGE: A package for automatic evaluation of summaries. In *Text Summarization Branches Out*, pages 74–81, Barcelona, Spain. Association for Computational Linguistics.

Fei Liu, Trevor Cohn, and Timothy Baldwin. 2018. Narrative modeling with memory chains and semantic supervision. In *Proceedings of the 56th Annual Meeting of the Association for Computational Linguistics (Volume 2: Short Papers)*, pages 278–284, Melbourne, Australia. Association for Computational Linguistics.

Yinhan Liu, Jiatao Gu, Naman Goyal, Xian Li, Sergey Edunov, Marjan Ghazvininejad, Mike Lewis, and Luke Zettlemoyer. 2020. Multilingual denoising pre-training for neural machine translation. *Transactions of the Association for Computational Linguistics*, 8:726–742.

Nasrin Mostafazadeh, Nathanael Chambers, Xiaodong He, Devi Parikh, Dhruv Batra, Lucy Vanderwende, Pushmeet Kohli, and James Allen. 2016. A corpus and cloze evaluation for deeper understanding of commonsense stories. In *Proceedings of the 2016 Conference of the North American Chapter of the Association for Computational Linguistics: Human Language Technologies*, pages 839–849, San Diego, California. Association for Computational Linguistics.

Erik T Mueller. 2004. Understanding script-based stories using commonsense reasoning. *Cognitive Systems Research*, 5(4):307–340.

Kishore Papineni, Salim Roukos, Todd Ward, and Wei-Jing Zhu. 2002. Bleu: a method for automatic evaluation of machine translation. In *Proceedings of the 40th Annual Meeting of the Association for Computational Linguistics*, pages 311–318, Philadelphia, Pennsylvania, USA. Association for Computational Linguistics.

Edoardo Maria Ponti, Goran Glavaš, Olga Majewska, Qianchu Liu, Ivan Vulić, and Anna Korhonen. 2020. XCOPA: A multilingual dataset for causal commonsense reasoning. In *Proceedings of the 2020 Conference on Empirical Methods in Natural Language Processing (EMNLP)*, pages 2362–2376, Online. Association for Computational Linguistics.

Melissa Roemmele, Cosmin Adrian Bejan, and Andrew S Gordon. 2011. Choice of plausible alternatives: An evaluation of commonsense causal reasoning. In *AAAI Spring Symposium: Logical Formalizations of Commonsense Reasoning*, pages 90–95.

Maarten Sap, Ronan Le Bras, Emily Allaway, Chandra Bhagavatula, Nicholas Lourie, Hannah Rashkin, Brendan Roof, Noah A Smith, and Yejin Choi. 2019. Atomic: An atlas of machine commonsense for if-then reasoning. In *Proceedings of the AAAI Conference on Artificial Intelligence*, pages 3027–3035.

Roy Schwartz, Maarten Sap, Ioannis Konstas, Leila Zilles, Yejin Choi, and Noah A. Smith. 2017. Story cloze task: UW NLP system. In *Proceedings of the 2nd Workshop on Linking Models of Lexical, Sentential and Discourse-level Semantics*, pages 52–55, Valencia, Spain. Association for Computational Linguistics.

Rishi Sharma, James Allen, Omid Bakhshandeh, and Nasrin Mostafazadeh. 2018. Tackling the story ending biases in the story cloze test. In *Proceedings of the 56th Annual Meeting of the Association for Computational Linguistics (Volume 2: Short Papers)*, pages 752–757, Melbourne, Australia. Association for Computational Linguistics.

Yoav Shoham. 1990. Nonmonotonic reasoning and causation. *Cognitive Science*, 14(2):213–252.

Jenny Thomas. 1983. Cross-cultural pragmatic failure. *Applied linguistics*, 4(2):91–112.

Thomas Wolf, Lysandre Debut, Victor Sanh, Julien Chaumond, Clement Delangue, Anthony Moi, Pierric Cistac, Tim Rault, Rémi Louf, Morgan Funtowicz, and Jamie Brew. 2019. Huggingface's transformers: State-of-the-art natural language processing. *arXiv preprint arXiv:1910.03771*.

Tianyi Zhang, Varsha Kishore, Felix Wu, Kilian Q. Weinberger, and Yoav Artzi. 2020. Bertscore: Evaluating text generation with bert. In *ICLR 2020 : Eighth International Conference on Learning Representations*.

A Training Configurations

A.1 Classification

For LSTM, we set the maximum token for each sentence to be 30, and train the model for 100 epochs with early stopping (patience = 20), a batch size of 20, Adam optimizer, and a learning rate of 0.01. For pretrained-language model, we set the maximum token to be 450 and 50 for the premise and ending sentence, respectively, and train the model for 20 epochs with early stopping (patience = 5), a batch size of 40, Adam optimizer, an initial learning rate of 5e-5, and warm-up of 10% of the total steps.

A.2 Generation

To train the sentence-5 generation task, we set the maximum length of tokens to be 200 and 50 for the input and target text, respectively. We train the models on $4 \times$V100 32GB GPUs for 60 epochs with an initial learning rate of 1e-4 (Adam optimizer). We use a total batch size of 320 (20 x 4 GPUs x gradient accumulation of 4), a warmup of 10% of total steps, and save checkpoints for every 500 steps. We also compute ROUGE scores (R1) to pick the best checkpoint based on the development set. For calculating BERTScore we use `bert-base-multilingual-cased` based on layer suggested by Zhang et al. (2020).

B Additional Data Statistics

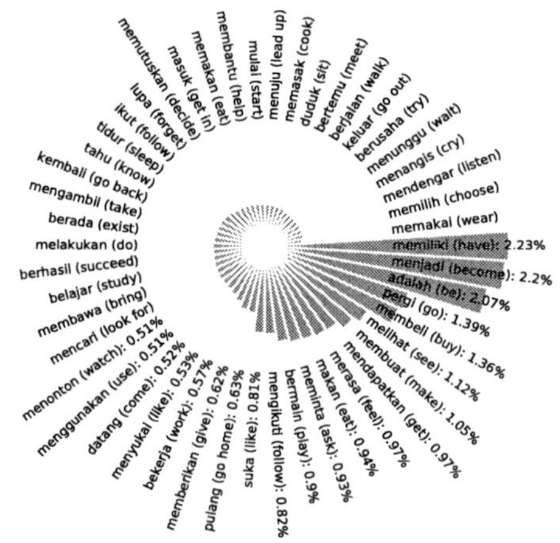

Figure 2: Distribution of top-50 verbs in our corpus.

C Analysis on Classification Task: FP and TP Samples

We further analyze false positive (FP) and true positive (TP) of INDOBERT by considering 1) whether the story contains temporal and causal relations; and 2) the number of premise sentences that are minimally required to entail the right ending.[12] We randomly selected 50 samples from each FP and TP sets, and found that 60% of FP samples have temporal relations while TP has lower percentage (56%). On the other hand, causal relations tends to be correctly predicted, with proportion 88% and 94% for FP and TP, respectively. Lastly,

[12]Sentence can be in any position.

we found that FP samples have a higher average of minimally-required premise: 2.8 (out of 4), while TP samples are only 2.1.

D Human Evaluations

Aspect	Kappa Score
A	0.59
B	0.49
C	0.75
D	0.40
E	0.80
F	0.59

Table 10: **Generation task**: Kappa scores (inter-annotator agreement) of manual evaluation for 4 models × 50 randomly sampled Indonesian test. We evaluate whether the fifth-sentence: **A**: does not contain repetition; **B**: follows commonsense; **C**: is a fluent Indonesian; **D**: has a good flow; **E**: has natural English code-switching; and **F**: has unnatural English code-switching.

Aspect	EN–ID		ID–EN	
	Adequacy	Fluency	Adequacy	Fluency
Pearson	0.55	0.56	0.39	0.37
Score	4.47	4.57	4.60	4.58

Table 11: **Classification task**: We randomly sample 100 sentences (of stories) and use Google Translate to obtain the translation. We ask two expert workers to evaluate adequacy and fluency of EN–ID and ID–EN translation (Koehn and Monz, 2006). Scores reflect the average of two annotations, ranging between 1–5.

E Interview Questions

Buatlah sebuah cerita pendek dengan 5 kalimat!

Cerita pendek yang kami maksud terdiri dari 4 kalimat dan 2 kalimat penutup. Satu kalimat penutup merupakan kalimat yang sesuai dengan logika manusia berdasarkan 4 kalimat premise (sesuai dengan commonsense), sedangan 1 kalimat penutup lainnya merupakan kalimat yang tidak sesuai dengan logika manusia (commonsense).

==== Contoh STORY-1 ====

1. Nenek sangat suka menonton sinetron
2. Tiap sore setelah sholat isya beliau duduk di depan layar televisi selama 3 jam
3. Sesekali beliau bergumam karena kesal melihat pemeran antagonis yang tingkahnya sering menjahati pemeran utama
4. Tak jarang nenek juga ditemani kakek ketika menonton sinetron

Correct ending (5): Bagi nenek sinetron menjadi sarana hiburannya di malam hari
Incorrect ending (5): Nenek sangat ingin menjadi salah satu pemeran sinetron dan akan syuting esok hari

==== Contoh STORY-2 ====

1. Pak Miskin punya 3 orang anak
2. Sinta anak pertama kelas 6 SD
3. Anak kedua bernama Heru berusia 4 tahun
4. Anak yang paling kecil bernama Cahyono

Correct ending (5): Ia masih berusia 10 bulan
Incorrect ending (5): Cahyono duduk di kelas 3 SD

Make a short story with 5 sentences!

The short story consists of 4 sentences and 2 ending sentences. One ending sentence is a sentence that is in accordance with human logic based on 4 premise sentences (follows the commonsense), while the other one is a sentence that is not in accordance with human logic (do not follow the commonsense).

==== Example-1 ====

1. Grandma really likes watching soap operas.
2. Every evening after evening prayer she sits in front of the television for 3 hours.
3. Sometimes she muttered because she was annoyed to see the antagonist.
4. Often, she is accompanied by her husband when watching soap operas

Correct ending (5): For my grandmother, soap operas are a good entertainment at night
Incorrect ending (5): Grandma really wants to be a soap opera actor and will shoot tomorrow

==== Example-2 ====

1. Pak Miskin has 3 children
2. Sinta, the first child is in grade 6.
3. The second child named Heru is 4 years old
4. The youngest child is Cahyono

Correct ending (5): He is still 10 months old
Incorrect ending (5): Cahyono is in grade 3.

Figure 3: Interview question that is used in the hiring of story writers. The second row is the English translation (for illustration).

F Examples of Sentence-5 Generation

Premise: *Sudah lima belas tahun Jerry tidak berkunjung ke SD tempatnya menuntut ilmu.* *Saat ia akan menikah, ia mengunjungi sekolahnya untuk memberikan undangan ke guru-gurunya.* *Saat bertemu mereka, ia merasa sangat terharu.* *Guru-guru yang mengajarnya saat SD, kini tidak lagi semuda dulu.* **Gold:** *Meski begitu, mereka masih ingat dengan Jerry dan kenakalannya semasa sekolah* **EN model:** *Jerry merasa kehilangan sekolah tempatnya menuntut ilmu* **ID model:** *Jerry senang sekali dengan keberadaan guru-gurunya* **EN+ID model:** *Jerry sangat bangga dengan tempatnya belajar ilmu*
Premise: It has been fifteen years that Jerry has not visited his elementary school. Today he is visiting his school to invite his teachers to his wedding. He feels so happy meeting with his former teachers. Those teachers are no longer as young as fifteen years ago. **Gold:** Even so, they still remember Jerry. **EN model:** Jerry feels that he has lost his school. **ID model:** Jerry is very happy with his teachers. **EN+ID model:** Jerry is very proud of his primary school.

Figure 4: Example of sentence-5 generation output using MBART model. The second row is the English translation (for illustration).

Psycholinguistic Diagnosis of Language Models' Commonsense Reasoning

Yan Cong
yancong222@gmail.com

Abstract

Neural language models have attracted a lot of attention in the past few years. More and more researchers are getting intrigued by how language models encode commonsense, specifically what kind of commonsense they understand, and why they do. This paper analyzed neural language models' understanding of commonsense pragmatics (i.e., implied meanings) through human behavioral and neurophysiological data. These psycholinguistic tests are designed to draw conclusions based on predictive responses in context, making them very well suited to test word-prediction models such as BERT in natural settings. They can provide the appropriate prompts and tasks to answer questions about linguistic mechanisms underlying predictive responses. This paper adopted psycholinguistic datasets to probe language models' commonsense reasoning. Findings suggest that GPT-3's performance was mostly at chance in the psycholinguistic tasks. We also showed that DistillBERT had some understanding of the (implied) intent that's shared among most people. Such intent is implicitly reflected in the usage of conversational implicatures and presuppositions. Whether or not fine-tuning improved its performance to human-level depends on the type of commonsense reasoning.

1 Introduction

In this paper, we focus on Language Models' (LMs) performance in commonsense reasoning tasks. Different from language semantics concerning logical relations between isolated sentence meanings, we take pragmatics to be sentences' relations relying on conversational participants' commonsense, such as the basic level *intent* that is commonly shared among most people. Humans reason about what their interlocutor could have said but chose not to, thereby drawing various inferences. The way humans put linguistic meanings to use depends on social interaction and commonsense assumption. What about machines whose pre-trainings do not involve social interaction? To what extent do they still have this pragmatic knowledge? How do they cooperate without any forms of learning in Grice pragmatics (Grice, 1975)? This paper attempts to answer these questions by examining transformer LMs' performance in commonsense reasoning.

We focus on two commonsense pragmatics phenomena: (i) Presupposition (henceforth Presp), for example, by using determiner *the* in the utterance "*the* teacher spoke to me" most people typically presuppose the existence of such a teacher in the context; (ii) Scalar Implicature (henceforth SI), for example, by using quantifier *some* in "I ate *some* of the cookies", most people generally imply "not all". We provided linguistic perspectives about how humans compute and evaluate commonsense pragmatics. We then assessed the extent to which LMs can understand the meanings pragmatically enriched by human speakers. Moreover, we fine-tuned LMs with pragmatic inference datasets. Evaluation comparisons are reported and discussed. We make all code and test data available for additional testing[1].

2 Related work

LMs' knowledge about syntax and semantics is relatively well studied (Warstadt et al., 2020; Tenney et al., 2019; Devlin et al., 2019). Considerably fewer studies have been done on speaker's intent: the implied meaning that's commonly shared among most people's intention. This is called Conversational Implicature in pragmatics literature (Grice, 1975). Implicature phenomena like quantifiers *some* and *many* are tested in recent studies (Schuster et al., 2020; Jeretic et al., 2020). The diagnostics in these studies are controlled. Most of them incorporate offline human responses to words in context such as acceptability judgment surveys.

Relatively few studies include online human response in the assessment (Ettinger, 2020). On-

[1] https://github.com/yancong222/Pragamtics-Commonsense-LMs

Proceedings of the First Workshop on Commonsense Representation and Reasoning (CSRR 2021), pages 17 - 22

line measurement uses neurolinguistic equipment electroencephalogram (EEG) and Event-Related-Potentials (ERP) to record brain activity (Luck, 2012). ERP components such as N400 wave is an event-related brain potential measured using EEG. N400 refers to a negativity peaking at about 400 milliseconds after stimulus onset. It has been used to investigate semantic processing. N400 is relevant because it's an online real-time measurement of human brain's response to different language phenomena, and it has been mostly elicited as a result of human processing sentences with semantic anomalies. Online measurement differs from offline judgments survey or cloze test in that online measurement reveals human brain's real-time sensitivity to (linguistic) cues. We examine LMs using human centered datasets that are collected through both offline and online experiments.

How "human-like" the state-of-the-art LMs are (cognitive plausibility) has not comprehensively justified (Wang et al., 2019). Goldstein et al. (2021) provides empirical evidence that the human brain and GPT-2 share fundamental computational principles as they process natural language. In a sense that both are engaged in continuous next-word prediction, and both represent words as a function of the previous context. Against this background, we study LMs' cognitive plausibility through examining their performance in understanding pragmatically enriched meanings, which are *implied* or *presupposed* among most people (i.e. conversational participants) to convey their intentions.

3 Experiments

We first designed most of the tests in the form of cloze tasks, so as to test the pre-trained LMs in their most natural setting, without interference from fine-tuning. The main schema we used in this study is called the *minimal pair paradigm*, in which two linguistic items are in contrastive distribution, meaning the two items are identical except one single aspect. The notion of *minimal pair* is widely used in linguistic experiments probing the underlying structures of a linguistic utterance. Typically, one of the two items is pragmatically *odd* according to most people's commonsense knowledge (marked by #), relative to the other utterance in the minimal pair.

The hypothesis and the accuracy calculation pipeline are as follows. If LMs understand commonsense intent, which gets reflected in the usage of SI and Presp, LMs should endorse more often the pragmatically good sentence than its pragmatically odd counterpart in a minimal pair. To quantify such "endorsement", we calculated the percentage p of cases in which LMs favor the pragmatically good sentence over the pragmatically odd one. The extent to which LMs (dis-)favor an sentence is derived from LMs' tokenized sequence log probability (henceforth logprob). The accuracy mean for each condition (*good* vs. *bad/so-so*) is then calculated per phenomenon (SI and Presp), using the sum of percentage p divided by the number of sentences, grouped by phenomenon. DistillBERT (Sanh et al., 2019) is used, which has only the *encoder* transformer, It's necessary that models are able to use right-hand context for word predictions. We compare DistillBERT with another type of LMs GPT-3 (Brown et al., 2020), which has only the *decoder*. We present model cards in Table (1).

Model	n_{params}	n_{layers}
DistillBERT-base-uncased	67M	6
GPT-3/InstructGPT	175.0B	96

Table 1: (pre-trained LMs) Model cards

Study 1: Presupposition Our first study is built up on Singh et al. (2016). They performed human behavioral acceptance judgment experiments using the presupposition triggers *the*. Participants were asked to drop out when they think the sentence stops making sense. Singh et al. (2016)'s findings show that humans think utterances make less sense relative to the controls when the presupposed information is implausible. We extracted 82 items from Singh et al. (2016) human experiments stimuli, which are already cognitively justified and freely available in their appendix. *Seth went to jail/ # a restaurant on Saturday night. The guard spoke to him there for a while.* presupposes that *there is a unique* guard in the context. Given commonsense world knowledge and the close association of guard and jail, "Seth went to jail" is a more likely and plausible context, thus "a restaurant" is marked with #. Utterance *Kristen went to a restaurant/ # jail in the morning. The waiter served her there quickly.* presupposes *the existence* of a (unique) waiter in the context. "Kristen went to a restaurant" is a better context in a sense that it lays out a background where there is a waiter. By contrast, jail is rarely associated with waiter, "went to jail" is implausible and is marked with #. It's both the uniqueness of the "waiter" and the relevance of the job to the place "restaurant" that affect the context. Singh et al. (2016) reported that in this stops-making-sense paradigm, human participants were near-ceiling in accepting plausible conditions: at the last region of the sentence, the acceptance rate was 95% in the plausible condition. For implausible *the*, by the end of the sentence, 50% dropped out since it stops making sense and most people cannot accept it.

Built up on Singh et al. (2016) human experiment, we evaluated LMs' sensitivity to Presp. We compared the accuracy mean of each condition, as exemplified in *John went to school on Monday afternoon. The substitute teacher spoke to him there briefly.* versus *John went to a concert on Monday afternoon. The substitute teacher spoke to him there briefly.*. The two utterances differ in only one element "school"/"concert". The former is pragmatically good relative to the latter, given that *the* presupposes a context where *there is* a teacher, and commonsense tells us that "teacher" and "school" are closer than "teacher" and "concert".

GPT-3 is evaluated by the extent to which it favors plausible cases over the implausible ones. Sequential word-by-word logprob is generated and transformed into percent. We take the sum of word level logprob averaged by sentence length to be a proxy to the sentence *naturalness*. Higher percent indicates that GPT-3 evaluates the sentence to be natural. DistillBERT is evaluated through critical word prediction. Noun phrase in the initial sentence is masked and taken as the critical word. (e.g., *school* is masked in "*John went to school. The substitute teacher spoke to him there briefly.*", whereas *concert* is masked in "*John went to a concert. The substitute teacher spoke to him there briefly.*". Given that human data shows preference to the plausible over the implausible, DistillBERT is considered to have succeeded if the critical word is in its top$K$ (K=5) tokens for the plausible sentence. It's also considered succeed if the critical word is NOT in BERT's top$K$ for the implausible sentence.

Study 2: Scalar Implicature According to Nieuwland et al. (2010), relative clauses can make implicatures unnoticed by most people in sentence processing. Table (2) shows that there is a pragmatic violation in (a) if conversation participant actively draws pragmatic inference that "some (but not all)" office buildings have desks. However, this violation is left unnoticed in (a) due to the presence of the relative clause. (c) is relatively bad and implausible compared to (d): the violation in (c) is noticed due to the absence of a relative clause. Note that Nieuwland et al. (2010) considered the Communication sub-scale of the Autism-Spectrum Quotient questionnaire (AQ) (Baron-Cohen et al., 1994, 2001; Baron-Cohen, 2008) to be a proxy to be an individual's pragmatic skills. According to Nieuwland et al. (2010), the AQ quantifies pragmatic capabilities on a continuum from autism to typicality.

Nieuwland et al. (2010) reported that only pragmatically skilled participants (i.e., lower autism scores) are sensitive to the pragmatic violation in (c) (r=-.53, p=0.003). For (a), in which the implicature is left unnoticed, so is the violation. There is thus no significant difference between the pragmatically skilled participants and those who have high autism scores (r=-.29, p=0.13). Overall pragmatically skilled people are good at generating robust pragmatic inferences that *some* implies *not all*, which gives rise to larger N400 when the utterance is pragmatically bad - N400 is a verified ERP elicited by anomaly stimuli (Luck, 2012).

We extracted 168 items from Nieuwland et al. (2010). Some examples of items from their data are "*Some people have lungs/pets, which require good care*". GPT-3 is used for sequential word prediction. Using sum of token level logprob averaged by sentence length, we examine if there is a difference with and without the SI being noticed. GPT-3 is considered succeed if the plausible sentence mean is higher (hence more favorable) than the soso/unacceptable sentence mean. We use masked language models like DistillBERT for critical word prediction. We masked quantifiers and take *some* as the critical word for (a,b,d). We take *all* as the critical word for (c), because SI is noticed and *all* is commonsense intent. Now that (a,b,c,d) are all not implausible, BERT is marked as succeed if the critical word is in its top*5* tokens list.

Sanity check One may wonder to what extent LM is merely leveraging nouns joint-probability. This motivates us to check whether the test datasets contain enough noun co-occurrence patterns that could make the LMs find a likelihood pattern rather than actually *reason* to conclude which sentence

Plausibility	Example	Label
So-so	(a) [Some] office buildings have *desks* that are covered with dust.	SI unnoticed
Plausible	(b) [Some] office buildings have *plants* that are covered with dust.	SI unnoticed
Implausible	(c) [Some] office buildings have *desks* and can become dusty.	SI noticed
Plausible	(d) [Some] office buildings have *plants* and can become dusty.	SI noticed

Table 2: Datasets and examples used in SI evaluation (Nieuwland et al., 2010)

is more plausible. For instance, the co-occurrence of *office-buildings* and *desks* in the SI *good* pair seems to be more frequently seen than that of *office-buildings* and *plants* in the *bad* pair, since plants are not essential, but desks are. Similarly, for the Presp stimuli, it appears that humans tend to associate *jail* with *guard* more frequently than they do so for *restaurant* and *guard*. To address these confounding factors, we use n-gram to calculate joint-probability (Yin et al., 2016). Results show that 70% of the SI and 50% of the Presp stimuli show higher co-occurrence probability in the 'good' sentence than in the 'bad' sentence[2].

4 Fine-tuning DistillBERT with ImpPres

In order to examine how to improve LMs' accuracy in these downstream tasks, and to further evaluate pre-trained LMs versus fine-tuned LMs, we fine-tuned DistillBERT-base-uncased with the ImpPress dataset (Jeretic et al., 2020). It consists of >25k semi-automatically generated sentence pairs illustrating well-studied commonsense pragmatic inference types. 14100 tagged utterance pairs were used in the training of Presp, and 1410 tagged pairs for testing. Here is the input representation: sentence 1 *Victoria's mall that has hurt Sam might upset Helen.*; sentence 2 *Victoria doesn't have exactly one mall that has hurt Sam.*; Label *contradiction.* As to SI, 6000 tagged utterance pairs were used for training and 600 for testing. Here is the input representation: sentence 1 *The teacher resembles some sketches.*; sentence 2 *The teacher doesn't resemble all sketches.*; Label *entailment.*

We fine-tuned DistillBERT-base-uncased on an Apple M1 CPU for 3 epochs. We used a batch size 64 of and optimized using Adam (Kingma and Ba, 2014) with betas=(0.9,0.999), with a learning rate of $2e$-05.

[2]This would seem to raise questions about the strength of the conclusions being drawn (c.f. section5) - it seems that LMs merely leverage co-occurrence frequency; on the other hand, it also appears that LMs' trend aligns with joint frequency - LMs does not fail the sanity check because frequency/prevalence heavily influences humans' commonsense reasoning too.

5 Evaluations and discussion

Error bar in Fig.1 shows DistillBERT does not seem to have difficulty detecting Presp, and fine-tuning slightly decreases its performance. This is likely due to the fact that Singh et al. (2016) data is not formatted the same as the ImpPress training data. Fine-tuning might have misled DistillBERT. Regarding SI, fine-tuning significantly increases LMs' performance, indicating that the ImpPress dataset is a good candidate for improving LMs' sensitivity to commonsense SIs. Error bar in Fig.2 indicates that GPT-3 is slightly better in detecting SI than in Presp, but overall GPT-3 is not good at the psycholinguistic task. This maybe because GPT-3 has a different architecture. LMs performance aligns with n-gram baseline in that overall the SI dataset is less challenging than the Presp: 70% of SI dataset shows the favorable co-occurrence direction: the pair tagged as 'good' also shows higher nouns co-occurrence rate than the 'bad' pair does. The Presp dataset is less helpful (50%).

It's worth noting that it's not clear if we can make a *direct* comparison between human decisions and LMs' rates, especially for the SI cases. Nieuwland et al. (2010) suggests that for humans, the informative and pragmatically good statements elicited larger N400 ERPs than underinformative and pragmatically bad statements. However, this does not directly transfer to the accuracy mean metric we used for LMs. All Fig.2 showed is that GPT-3's performance is roughly at chance, with respect to accuracy mean. For future studies, we plan to conduct parallel human studies to collect baseline human decision rates.

Regarding LMs evaluation analysis, our study shows that in order to probe commonsense knowledge from LMs, understand their reasoning mechanisms, and identify their limitations for AI applications due to the lack of commonsense knowledge, we need to carefully consider how to prompt the pre-trained LMs. For masked LMs such as DistillBERT, our results suggest that an appropriate method to examine how 'human-like' LMs are is to mask the same token as psycholinguists do in their behavioral/neural experiments with humans, and keep the same contextual information, so that the experiment setting is as close to human experiments as possible. As to unidirectional LMs like GPT-3, they read in sentence using almost the same fundamental mechanisms as humans do, we thus took sentence to be a unit to derive logprob. How much GPT-3 like the sentence is directly reflected in its sentence logprob. It's crucial to use different metrics for BERT and GPT-3 to avoid the pitfall of comparing the two with the same metrics, as they are trained very differently, and a perplexity comparison would be inconclusive.

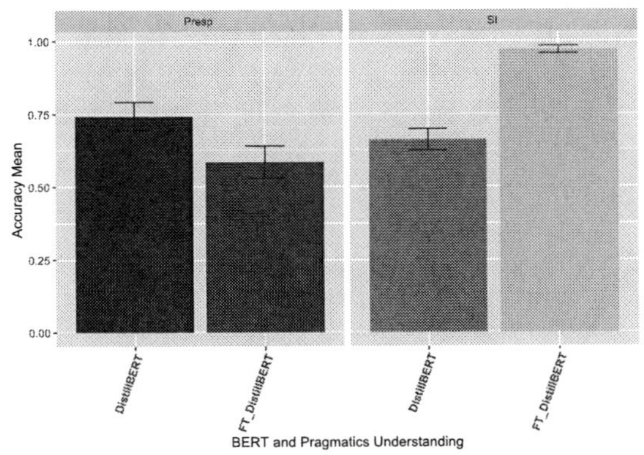

Figure 1: Evaluate BERT with human data. DistillBERT is used for critical word prediction. FT: fine-tuned.

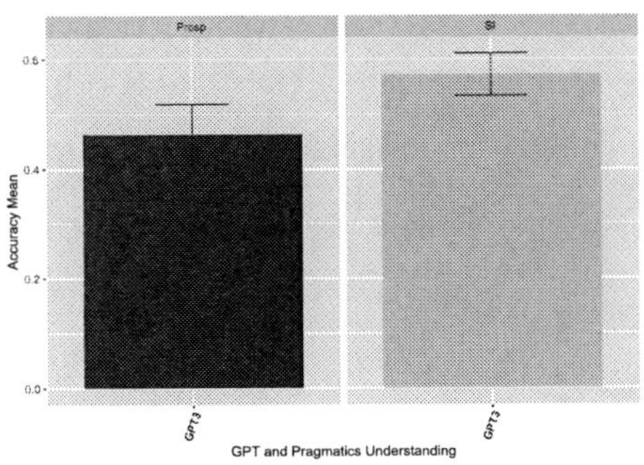

Figure 2: Evaluate GPT-3 with human data. GPT-3 is used for sequential word prediction.

Our study has some limitations. Although we mention multiple times that these pragmatics often exist in conversations, the actual datasets we used are not conversational. For future work, we hope to see how LMs perform in a conversation scenario in terms of commonsense pragmatics. This could give us a better grasp of LMs' competence at the conversational level of language understanding. For the current work, our motivation of using non-conversational human data for conversational implicature is that LMs are not trained the same way through many *dialogues*, but rather with text found on the web. Additionally, we acknowledge that there were some glitches in DistillBERT's SI evaluation setting. BERT is considered succeed as long as the critical word is in its top*K*. By not penalizing that *some* can be above *all* in the case where both would be in the top*K* choices, we accept LM's choice as "correct" white it isn't. It's also not very surprising that *all* doesn't show up as much as other options in BERT's top*K* choices for scenarios that *all* is the commonsense intent, given that LM might generate adjectives but not quantifiers to modify the following noun. It's likely that this has nothing to do with the implication, nevertheless they still make sense considering that the LM's learning algorithm uses masked loss. For future research, we hope to get more valid conclusions through directly comparing whether *all* is relatively more likely than *some*.

Humans show no difficulty in using commonsense knowledge to reason about daily conversations. By contrast, the extent to which LMs are sensitive to commonsense reasoning has remained an elusive research question in AI research for decades. Here, we provide an approach for commonsense reasoning tasks: incorporating online and offline psycholinguistic datasets into LMs evaluation. Using well-controlled task design and high resolution neurophysiology equipment, psycholinguistics studies all kinds of implicit meanings in natural language. To examine how 'human-like' LMs can be, human data is the key. These methods can improve the interpretability and explainability of neural models for reasoning about implied yet commonsense message.

To sum up, our paper aims to evaluate DistillBERT and GPT-3's ability to make human-like pragmatic inferences, such as SI and Presp, through human behavioral and neural data. Findings show psycholinguistic datasets can help get a good grasp of LMs' accuracy in detecting commonsense reasoning. Our study adopted a theory-supported lens for investigating the often vaguely-defined "commonsense", and illustrated how to establish connection between commonsense reasoning in NLP and pragmatic semantics.

References

Simon Baron-Cohen. 2008. Autism, hypersystemizing, and truth. Quarterly Journal of Experimental Psychology, 61(1):64–75.

Simon Baron-Cohen, Sally Wheelwright, Richard Skinner, Joanne Martin, and Emma Clubley. 2001. The autism-spectrum quotient (aq): Evidence from asperger syndrome/high-functioning autism, malesand females, scientists and mathematicians. Journal of autism and developmental disorders, 31(1):5–17.

Simon Ed Baron-Cohen, Helen Ed Tager-Flusberg, and Donald J Cohen. 1994. Understanding other minds: Perspectives from autism. In Most of the chapters in this book were presented in draft form at a workshop in Seattle, Apr 1991. Oxford University Press.

Tom Brown, Benjamin Mann, Nick Ryder, Melanie Subbiah, Jared D Kaplan, Prafulla Dhariwal, Arvind Neelakantan, Pranav Shyam, Girish Sastry, Amanda Askell, et al. 2020. Language models are few-shot learners. Advances in neural information processing systems, 33:1877–1901.

Jacob Devlin, Ming-Wei Chang, Kenton Lee, and Kristina Toutanova. 2019. BERT: Pre-training of deep bidirectional transformers for language understanding. In Proceedings of the 2019 Conference of the North American Chapter of the Association for Computational Linguistics: Human Language Technologies, Volume 1 (Long and Short Papers), pages 4171–4186, Minneapolis, Minnesota. Association for Computational Linguistics.

Allyson Ettinger. 2020. What BERT is not: Lessons from a new suite of psycholinguistic diagnostics for language models. Transactions of the Association for Computational Linguistics, 8:34–48.

Ariel Goldstein, Zaid Zada, Eliav Buchnik, Mariano Schain, Amy Price, Bobbi Aubrey, Samuel A Nastase, Amir Feder, Dotan Emanuel, Alon Cohen, et al. 2021. Thinking ahead: spontaneous prediction in context as a keystone of language in humans and machines. bioRxiv, pages 2020–12.

H.P. Grice. 1975. Syntax and Semantics, volume 3, chapter Logic and Conversation. Academic Press, New York.

Paloma Jeretic, Alex Warstadt, Suvrat Bhooshan, and Adina Williams. 2020. Are natural language inference models IMPPRESsive? Learning IMPlicature and PRESupposition. In Proceedings of the 58th Annual Meeting of the Association for Computational Linguistics, pages 8690–8705, Online. Association for Computational Linguistics.

Diederik P Kingma and Jimmy Ba. 2014. Adam: A method for stochastic optimization. arXiv preprint arXiv:1412.6980.

Steven J Luck. 2012. Event-related potentials.

Mante S. Nieuwland, Tali Ditman, and Gina R. Kuperberg. 2010. On the incrementality of pragmatic processing: An erp investigationof informativeness and pragmatic abilities. Journal of Memory and Language, 63:324–346.

Victor Sanh, Lysandre Debut, Julien Chaumond, and Thomas Wolf. 2019. Distilbert, a distilled version of bert: smaller, faster, cheaper and lighter. arXiv preprint arXiv:1910.01108.

Sebastian Schuster, Yuxing Chen, and Judith Degen. 2020. Harnessing the linguistic signal to predict scalar inferences. In Proceedings of the 58th Annual Meeting of the Association for Computational Linguistics, pages 5387–5403, Online. Association for Computational Linguistics.

Raj Singh, Evelina Fedorenko, Kyle Mahowald, and Edward Gibson. 2016. Accommodating presuppositions is inappropriate in implausible contexts. Cognitive Science, 40:607–634.

Ian Tenney, Dipanjan Das, and Ellie Pavlick. 2019. BERT rediscovers the classical NLP pipeline. In Proceedings of the 57th Annual Meeting of the Association for Computational Linguistics, pages 4593–4601, Florence, Italy. Association for Computational Linguistics.

Alex Wang, Yada Pruksachatkun, Nikita Nangia, Amanpreet Singh, Julian Michael, Felix Hill, Omer Levy, and Samuel Bowman. 2019. Superglue: A stickier benchmark for general-purpose language understanding systems. Advances in neural information processing systems, 32.

Alex Warstadt, Alicia Parrish, Haokun Liu, Anhad Mohananey, Wei Peng, Sheng-Fu Wang, and Samuel R. Bowman. 2020. BLiMP: A benchmark of linguistic minimal pairs for English. In Proceedings of the Society for Computation in Linguistics 2020, pages 409–410, New York, New York. Association for Computational Linguistics.

Wenpeng Yin, Hinrich Schütze, Bing Xiang, and Bowen Zhou. 2016. Abcnn: Attention-based convolutional neural network for modeling sentence pairs. Transactions of the Association for Computational Linguistics, 4:259–272.

Bridging the Gap between Recognition-level Pre-training and Commonsensical Vision-language Tasks

Yue Wan*, **Yueen Ma***, **Haoxuan You**, **Zhecan Wang**, **Shih-Fu Chang**
Columbia University
{yw3373, ym2745, hy2612, zw2627, sc250}@columbia.edu

Abstract

Large-scale visual-linguistic pre-training aims to capture the generic representations from multimodal features, which are essential for downstream vision-language tasks. Existing methods mostly focus on learning the semantic connections between visual objects and linguistic content, which tend to be recognition-level information and may not be sufficient for commonsensical reasoning tasks like VCR. In this paper, we propose a novel commonsensical vision-language pre-training framework to bridge the gap. We first augment the conventional image-caption pre-training datasets with commonsense inferences from a visual-linguistic GPT-2. To pre-train models on image, caption and commonsense inferences together, we propose two new tasks: *masked commonsense modeling* (MCM) and *commonsense type prediction* (CTP). To reduce the shortcut effect between captions and commonsense inferences, we further introduce the *domain-wise adaptive masking* that dynamically adjusts the masking ratio. Experimental results on downstream tasks, VCR and VQA, show the improvement of our pre-training strategy over previous methods. Human evaluation also validates the relevance, informativeness, and diversity of the generated commonsense inferences. Overall, we demonstrate the potential of incorporating commonsense knowledge into the conventional recognition-level visual-linguistic pre-training.

1 Introduction

Vision-language multimodal tasks have received vast attention in the deep learning field in recent years. Tasks, like Visual Question Answering (VQA) (Antol et al., 2015; Goyal et al., 2017) and Visual Commonsense Reasoning (VCR) (Zellers et al., 2019), require different levels of multimodal reasoning ability to make task-specific decisions.

*These authors contributed equally. The majority of this work is finished during their master's degree at Columbia University.

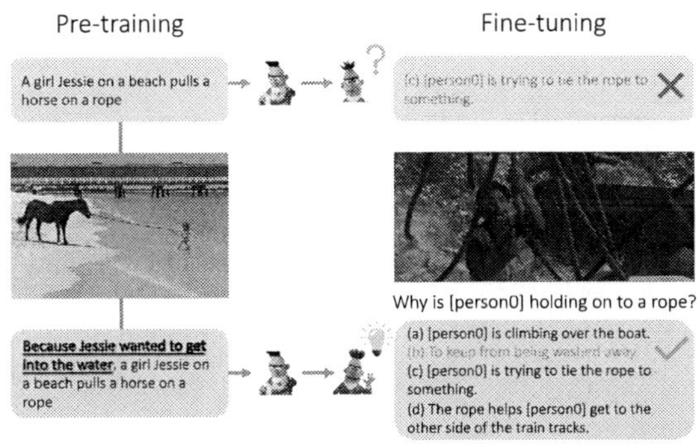

Figure 1: An example of our commonsensical visual-linguistic pre-training (bottom) compared against the conventional visual-linguistic pre-training (top). Commonsensical knowledge (e.g., the bold underlined text) is generated and learned by models during our commonsensical pre-training. Such knowledge becomes useful for downstream commonsense reasoning tasks: our model correctly answers the question while the conventional method is wrong.

Motivated by the advancement of pre-training in both computer vision (CV), such as backbone networks pre-trained on ImageNet (Deng et al., 2009), and natural language processing (NLP), such as BERT (Devlin et al., 2018) and GPT-2 (Radford et al., 2019), numerous visual-linguistic pre-training strategies were proposed to learn the generic feature representations for vision-language tasks. Most of them (Su et al., 2020; Lu et al., 2019a; Chen et al., 2020; Tan and Bansal, 2019; Gan et al., 2020) take advantage of large-scale image captioning datasets, such as Conceptual Captions (Sharma et al., 2018) and MSCOCO Captions (Lin et al., 2014). These pre-training tasks mostly focus on learning the modality alignments between regions-of-interest (RoIs) from images and words from captions by applying the visual-linguistic extensions of the *masked language modeling* (MLM) objective. There are also other multimodal objectives, such as *word-region alignment* (Lu et al., 2019a; Chen et al., 2020), *image-text matching* (Chen et al., 2020) and *scene graph prediction* (Yu

Proceedings of the First Workshop on Commonsense Representation and Reasoning (CSRR 2021), pages 23 - 35
May 27, 2022

	Recognition-level	Commonsensical	
Type	Low-level Caption	Commonsense Inference	High-level Caption
Dataset	MSCOCO	VisualCOMET	Ours
Example	A girl Jessie on a beach pulls a horse on a rope	<intent> **get into the water**	Because Jessie wanted to **get into the water**, a girl Jessie on a beach pulls a horse on a rope.

Table 1: Terminologies used in this paper, along with their corresponding datasets and examples. The bold text represents the commonsense inference and the underlined text represents template tokens for the commonsense type, <intent>. The example captions correspond to the left image in Figure 1.

(a) Recognition-level VQA Example.
Q: What are the people racing?
A: Horses.

(b) Commonsensical VQA Example.
Q: Why are the men jumping?
A: To catch frisbee.

(c) VCR Example (Commonsensical).
Q: Why is [person4] pointing at [person1]?
A: He is telling [person3] that [person1] ordered the pancakes.

Figure 2: Recognition-level and commonsensical visual question answering examples from VQA and VCR.

et al., 2020).

Despite the variety of those proposed pre-training strategies, they mostly capture the recognition-level relationship between the two modalities, which might not be sufficient for vision-language tasks that require cognition-level reasoning abilities. Here, the term *cognition* is taken from VCR to represent reasoning abilities and is more advanced than *recognition*. In this work, we rephrase *cognition-level* as *commonsensical* to avoid confusion. As an example, being aware of the word "man" referring to the human-alike object in the image is insufficient to infer his future behavior. Su et al. (2020); Chen et al. (2020) also showed the similar discrepancy between recognition-level pre-training and commonsensical fine-tuning. Thus, the motivation of this work is to bridge the gap between the two learning stages for vision-language reasoning tasks.

Not to be confused with the term "commonsense" described in CommonsenseQA (Talmor et al., 2019), we approach it from a cognitive perspective and take the concept of "commonsense inference" proposed in VisualCOMET (Park et al., 2020) as the starting point. It introduced three specific types of commonsense knowledge, which are the possible incidents before or after the current event (i.e., temporal), and the potential intentions of the target subjects (i.e., intentional). Unfortunately, these information does not normally exist in conventional captions. Therefore, a natural question would be whether introducing additional commonsense knowledge in pre-training can further improve upon the downstream commonsensical tasks.

To answer this question, we develop a novel commonsensical vision-language pre-training framework, which contains two main components: (1) Generating commonsense inferences for the conventional image-caption dataset; (2) Introducing suitable pre-training strategies for image, caption, and commonsense inference together.

As for commonsense inference generation, we fine-tune a visual-linguistic GPT-2 on VisualCOMET (Park et al., 2020) as our commonsense generator and infer the temporal and intentional commonsense for the image-caption pairs in MSCOCO dataset. We define the conventional captions such as MSCOCO captions as the *low-level* captions. We then combine the low-level captions with the commonsense inferences using pre-defined templates to get the *high-level* captions. The terminologies used in this paper are collected in Table 1 and examples are shown in Figure 2.

Given additional commonsense inferences besides the image and caption, the pre-training strategy is the key to bridge the recognition-level information and commonsense. In short, we replace the low-level captions used in most conventional pre-training methods with the high-level captions. We propose two tasks toward commonsense inferences: *masked commonsense modeling* (MCM) and *commonsense type prediction* (CTP). MCM requires the model to predict the commonsense inference masked by the *domain-wise adaptive masking* strategy. It dynamically adjusts the masking ratio based on the semantic similarity between commonsense inferences and captions, for the sake of avoiding obvious shortcuts. In CTP, the type of commonsense among <intent>, <before> or <after> is predicted without knowing the template tokens, which forces the model to learn global relationships among commonsense, captions, and images.

Eventually, we take VCR and VQA as two downstream evaluation tasks to demonstrate the effectiveness of our framework. We further provide qualitative analysis and human evaluation to reveal the insights behind it.

Our main contributions in this paper are:

- We propose a novel commonsensical visual-linguistic pre-training framework for incorporating commonsense knowledge into the conventional image-caption pre-training;
- We fine-tune a visual-linguistic GPT-2 model as the commonsense generator that takes as input a low-level image-caption pair;
- We develop two commonsensical pre-training tasks—MCM and CTP, which encourages the model to internalize commonsensical reasoning ability;
- We conduct comprehensive comparison and ablation study to show that our pre-training framework leads to improvements of 1.43% on VCR and 1.26% on VQA. Moreover, a human evaluation is conducted to validate the quality of the generated commonsense inferences.

2 Related Work

2.1 Visual-linguistic Model

Vision and language models have been advancing rapidly and, with the introduction of Faster R-CNN (Ren et al., 2015) and Transformer-based models (Vaswani et al., 2017) (e.g., GPT (Radford et al., 2018, 2019; Brown et al., 2020) and BERT (Devlin et al., 2018)), many vision-language tasks are becoming easier to solve. The original BERT can be easily extended to vision-language multimodal settings by concatenating the visual features of regions-of-interest (RoIs) and linguistic features of word tokens. Multiple BERT variants were introduced to solve the *visual question answering* tasks in the past few years and they can be grouped into two categories: single-stream cross-modal Transformers and two-stream cross-modal Transformers. Single-stream Transformers (Su et al., 2020; Chen et al., 2020; Li et al., 2019; Huang et al., 2019) have only one encoder. The visual features and the linguistic features are concatenated together into a single input sequence. On the other hand, two-stream Transformers (Lu et al., 2019b; Yu et al., 2020; Tan and Bansal, 2019) have two independent encoders, one for the visual feature stream and the other one for the linguistic feature stream. Then a third encoder is used to capture the cross-modal relationship between the two modalities.

2.2 Visual-linguistic Pre-training

Visual-linguistic pre-training is widely applied to multimodal tasks using large-scale image captioning datasets, such as Conceptual Captions (Sharma et al., 2018) and MSCOCO (Lin et al., 2014). Two common pre-training tasks are *masked language modeling with visual clues* (MLM) and *masked RoI classification with linguistic clues* (MRC) (Su et al., 2020), which are the extensions of the original MLM task from BERT. *Word-region alignment* (Lu et al., 2019a; Chen et al., 2020), *image-text matching* (Chen et al., 2020), and *RoI feature regression* (Tan and Bansal, 2019) were also proposed. ERNIE-ViL (Yu et al., 2020) proposed the *scene graph prediction* task based on the semantic graphs parsed from the captions.

Other approaches for improving visual question answering performance were also proposed in addition to visual-linguistic pre-training. Wu et al. (2019) proposed to generate question-relevant captions jointly with answering the VQA questions. Kim and Bansal (2019) proposed to fuse the image, question, and answer inputs with an additional paragraph that provides a diverse and abstract description of the image. A similar idea is found in (Li et al., 2018) where generated captions are used to explain the image and combined with the question to produce more accurate answers. A detailed study (Singh et al., 2020) investigated the effect of the similarity between pre-training and fine-tuning datasets.

3 Our Method

3.1 Commonsense Inference Generation

Prior to our pre-training, we first generate commonsense inferences from the conventional image-caption pairs. In addition to the image domain and the caption domain, commonsense inferences are treated as a third knowledge domain that is required for our proposed pre-training. We take a visual-

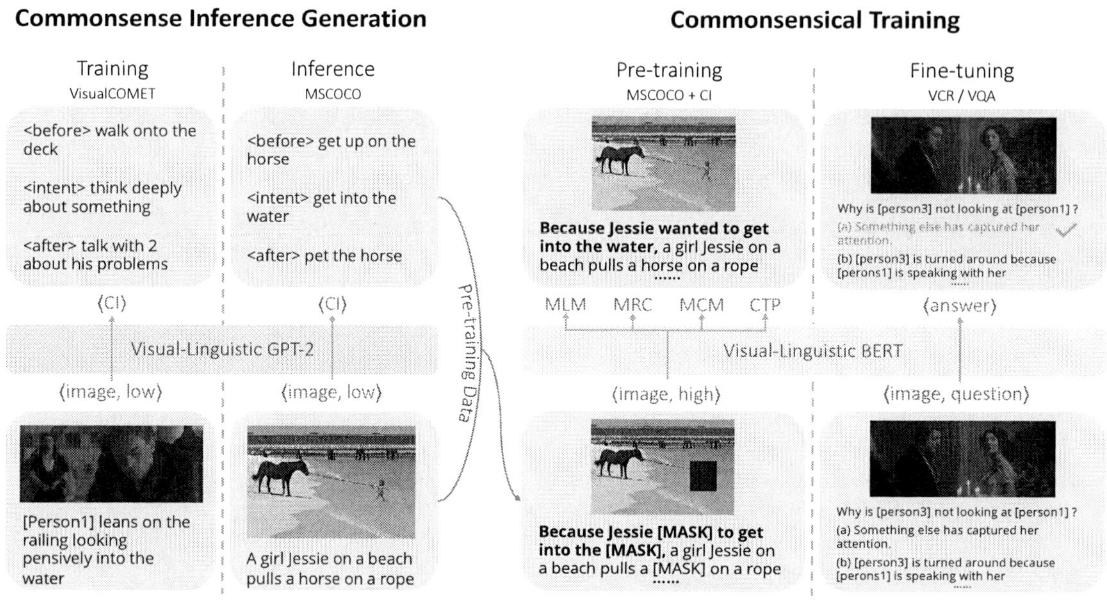

Figure 3: An overview of our commonsensical pre-training framework. The left part shows the commonsense inference generator; the right part shows the pre-training and fine-tuning pipelines. The bold text in the pre-training stage is the generated commonsense inference (CI) and the template tokens. The blue arrows point from the inputs to the target outputs. That is, the bottom images and sentences are the inputs while the top images and sentences are the objectives. "Low" and "high" stand for low-level captions and high-leval captions, respectively.

linguistic GPT-2 as the commonsense generator and fine-tune it on the VisualCOMET (Park et al., 2020) dataset. VisualCOMET introduces three specific types of commonsense inferences given the images and the captions (termed as <event>), which are the possible incidents before or after the current event (<before>, <after>) and the potential intentions of the people in the image (<intent>). Different from the GPT-2 model proposed in VisualCOMET that requires additional location information, our GPT-2 only takes image and caption as inputs, as shown in the left half of Figure 3. In general, it can be easily applied to any existing large-scale image captioning dataset. In this paper, we generate commonsense inferences for the image-caption pairs in MSCOCO (Lin et al., 2014). Appendix A.3 includes more details about how our GPT-2 model is fine-tuned. Instead of simply concatenating the features from the three knowledge domains, captions and commonsense inferences are combined by a set of pre-defined templates. We term the combined sequence as the *high-level* caption. An example is shown in Table 1 and template details are included in Appendix A.4.

3.2 Commonsensical Pre-training

To exploit the additional knowledge inside the commonsense inferences, we introduce a novel commonsensical pre-training strategy, which consists of two new tasks: *masked commonsense modeling* (MCM) and *commonsense type prediction* (CTP). Both tasks are proposed to learn commonsense from a fine-grained and global aspect, alongside the conventional *masked language modeling with visual clues* (MLM) and *masked RoI classification with linguistic clues* (MRC). In MCM, instead of the random masking used in previous works (Su et al., 2020; Chen et al., 2020; Tan and Bansal, 2019; Devlin et al., 2018), we propose the *domain-wise adaptive masking* to adjust the masking ratio according to the semantic similarity between commonsense inferences and captions. We detail them one by one below.

Masked Commonsense Modeling By incorporating commonsense inferences as the third knowledge domain additional to images and captions, we propose *masked commonsense modeling*. It is an extension of MLM with commonsense inferences as the input data and the *domain-wise adaptive masking* as the masking strategy. Each commonsense token is masked out by a probability that is controlled by the strategy detailed in the following "Domain-wise Adaptive Masking" subsection. The masked commonsense token c_m is replaced with the special token [MASK]. The model aims to predict c_m given the unmasked commonsense content

$c_{\backslash m}$ as well as the visual tokens v and linguistic tokens w by minimizing the negative log-likelihood:

$$\mathcal{L}_{\text{MCM}}(\theta) = -\mathbb{E}_{(c,w,v)\sim D} \log P_\theta(c_m|c_{\backslash m}, w, v)$$

where θ is the model parameters, and D is the training dataset. We argue that the introduction of commonsense knowledge will help the model gain commonsensical reasoning ability.

For image regions and linguistic tokens, inheriting from previous works (Lu et al., 2019a; Su et al., 2020; Chen et al., 2020), we still use MLM and MRC tasks. One slight difference is that our MLM/MRC task is conditioned on both commonsense clues and visual/linguistic clues.

Domain-wise Adaptive Masking Since commonsense inferences are generated from low-level image-caption pairs by a commonsensical GPT-2, captions and commonsense inferences are likely to be semantically related to each other. It means that the model could potentially take the shortcut by excessively relying on the low-level captions when predicting the masked commonsense tokens and vice versa, which makes MLM and MCM easier to solve. Below is an example where [MASK]$_4$ is more likely be to predicted as "bridge" based on the linguistic clues of "overlooking the river" rather than visual clues, because "bridge" and "river" often coexist in a sentence:

> *"Before a man Casey in a wheelchair and another* [MASK]$_1$ *on a bench* [MASK]$_2$ [MASK]$_3$ *overlooking the river ,* ***Casey needed to walk onto the*** [MASK]$_4$."

To tackle this issue, we introduce the *domain-wise adaptive masking* strategy. In conventional settings, each linguistic token has a probability of 15% to be masked. Domain-wise adaptive masking considers the semantic distance between commonsense inferences and low-level captions and computes the masking ratio accordingly. It takes the sentence embeddings of commonsense inferences and low-level captions from a pre-trained BERT (Devlin et al., 2018) and calculates their cosine similarity. The similarity score is passed to a logistic function and rescaled to a high probability interval. We pick the rescaling interval $(0.5, 1.0)$ to ensure high masking ratio. A higher semantic similarity between the low-level caption and the commonsense inference leads to a higher masking ratio on either the low-level captions or the commonsense inferences. Thus, the masking ratio is "adaptive" with respect to the embedding similarity. Detailed formulae and examples are shown in Appendix A.5.

During pre-training, adaptive masking is randomly applied on either low-level captions or commonsense inferences. Therefore, it is "domain-wise". When domain-wise adaptive masking is applied on low-level captions, it encourages the model to focus more on the visual clues for MCM. When domain-wise adaptive masking is applied on commonsense inferences, the same idea follows for MLM. The high masking ratio reduces the salience of one domain and elicits more advanced reasoning abilities, such as directly inferring commonsense knowledge from the images with only a few linguistic clues (heavily masked low-level captions).

Commonsense Type Prediction We also introduce a novel task of *commonsense type prediction* (CTP). It is an additional classification task that predicts the commonsense type (<intent>, <before> or <after>). Note that the template tokens are forced to be masked out in CTP since they are essentially the indicators of commonsense type. We also include the language modeling objective of these masked tokens in CTP. In general, it requires the model to perform commonsensical inference on the global relationship between commonsense and image-caption pairs.

4 Experiments

4.1 Implementation Details

GPT-2 is fine-tuned on VisualCOMET for 5 epochs using the AdamW optimizer with a learning rate of 5.0×10^{-5}. In pre-training and fine-tuning, we use the VL-BERT$_{\text{BASE}}$ configuration (Su et al., 2020), which is a single-stream cross-modal Transformer. VL-BERT is pre-trained for 10 epochs using the AdamW optimizer with a learning rate of 1.0×10^{-7} and a weight decay of 0.0001. For downstream task evaluation on VCR, the pre-trained VL-BERT is fine-tuned for 20 epochs using the SGD optimizer with a learning rate of 7.0×10^{-5} and a weight decay of 0.0001. For downstream task evaluation on VQA, the pre-trained VL-BERT is fine-tuned for 20 epochs using the AdamW optimizer with a learning rate of 6.25×10^{-7} and a weight decay of 0.0001. Our experiments are conducted on 4 Nvidia TITAN RTX GPUs.

Pre-training	VCR Q→A	VQA($_{v2}$) test-std	test-dev	val-human
None	70.00	69.03	68.85	63.43
Recognition-level	70.46 (+0.46)	69.95 (+0.92)	69.71 (+0.86)	66.09 (+2.66)
Commonsensical	**71.43** (+1.43)	**70.29** (+1.26)	**69.97** (+1.12)	**66.46** (+3.03)

Table 2: Performance (accuracy) comparison on VCR and VQA among 3 settings: fine-tuning from scratch, fine-tuning from recognition-level pre-training, and fine-tuning from commonsensical pre-training. "Q→A" represents the question answering task from the validation set of VCR; "test-std" and "test-dev" represents the two testing phases of VQA; "val-human" represents the human-centric validation set of VQA.

4.2 Datasets

Pre-training We take MSCOCO (Lin et al., 2014) as our low-level image captioning dataset and apply our fine-tuned GPT-2 model on it to generate commonsense inferences. To avoid noisy labeling, we only augment the image-caption pairs which depict humans since it is counter-intuitive to infer intentions for non-human objects. Then commonsense inferences and low-level captions are combined by a set of pre-defined templates to form high-level captions.

Fine-tuning To evaluate the effectiveness of our commonsensical pre-training, we use Visual Commonsense Reasoning (VCR) (Zellers et al., 2019) and Visual Question Answer v2.0 (VQA_{v2}) (Goyal et al., 2017) for downstream task evaluation. The overall task of VCR is to select the correct answer (A) as well as the rationale (R) given an image-question (Q) pair. Existing works (Lu et al., 2019a; Su et al., 2020; Chen et al., 2020; Tan and Bansal, 2019; Yu et al., 2020) have shown that Q→A is a more challenging task, which is what we use to evaluate our proposed pre-training framework. VQA_{v2} is another visual question answering task, where it primarily targets recognition-level understanding. In addition to the test set, we also evaluate our pre-training on a validation subset of VQA_{v2}, where only images that depict humans are considered. We term this subset as the human-centric VQA. We argue that these image-question pairs are more likely to be commonsensical (e.g., why is person...?). The subset is selected by the keyword matching of VQA's corresponding MSCOCO captions by a pre-defined human entity dictionary (e.g., student, firefighter).

4.3 Downstream Task Evaluation

To demonstrate the effectiveness of our pre-training framework, we fine-tune VL-BERT with different pre-train settings on VCR and VQA, including VL-BERT without pre-training, VL-BERT with conventional (i.e., recognition-level) pre-training, and VL-BERT with our commonsensical pre-training. Table 2 shows their performance comparison of accuracy on downstream tasks.

VCR The 1.43% performance increase on VCR from the no pre-training setting indicates the effectiveness of our proposed method and, in turn, the advantage of incorporating commonsense knowledge in pre-training. The slight 0.46% performance increase made by the conventional image-caption pre-training is consistent with the findings in VL-BERT and UNITER that the recognition-level pre-training might not be sufficient for commonsensical reasoning tasks. Our commonsensical pre-training enabled a 0.97% improvement over the recognition-level pre-training.

VQA As for VQA_{v2}, there is a 1.26% performance increase from no pre-training to our commonsensical pre-training in test-std set and a 1.12% increase in test-dev set. Our pre-training also improves over the conventional image-caption pre-training by 0.34% and 0.28%, respectively. Such increments are slightly smaller when compared to that on VCR. The reasone is that the questions in VQA mostly target recognition-level understanding (e.g., *What color is the ...?*, *What is the ...?*, *How many ...?*), the gap between recognition-level pre-training and fine-tuning on VQA is much smaller than that on VCR. In other words, commonsensical pre-training might be less necessary for VQA. On the other hand, the performance increment in the human-centric VQA is larger, at 0.37%. The comparison of no pre-training settings between "val-human" and the remaining VQA set (Table 2) has shown that human-centric VQA is a more challenging problem than the general VQA.

The performance gap between our results and the reported results from previous works (Su et al., 2020) is expected since our pre-training dataset is much smaller than the commonly used massive image-caption datasets, such as Conceptual Captions (Sharma et al., 2018). We also did not perform any hyperparameter tuning for the visual-linguistic BERT or fine-tuning of the image feature extractor Faster R-CNN, since we are aiming for rela-

Pre-training	VCR Acc. (Q→A)
(a) None	70.00
(b) MLM_{rec}	70.46
(c) MLM_{rec} (Aug. + Rand-1 + DAM)	70.55
(d) MLM_{rec} + MCM (Top-1)	70.32
(e) MLM_{rec} + MCM (Rand-1)	70.60
(f) MLM_{rec} + MCM (Rand-1 + DAM)	71.02
(g) MLM_{rec} + MCM (Rand-1 + DAM) + CTP	71.43

Table 3: Comparison of individual component of our proposed pre-training on VCR. MLM_{rec}: recognition-level pre-training tasks, including MLM and MRC; Top-1: pre-train using the top-1 commonsense inference from our fine-tuned GPT-2; Rand-1: pre-train using one commonsense inference randomly selected from the five candidates at each iteration; MCM: *masked commonsense modeling*; DAM: *domain-wise adaptive masking* strategy; CTP: *commonsense type prediction* task.

tive performance comparison rather than absolute improvement with respect to the state-of-the-art models.

4.4 Ablation Study

We further conduct a comprehensive ablation study to analyze the effect of each component in our commonsensical pre-training, as shown in Table 3. The ablation study is on VCR because we are more interested in commonsensical tasks and VCR is specifically designed for that.

The improvement from (d) to (e) indicates that the diversity of commonsense knowledge benefits the learning. When comparing (e) against (b), we can conclude that our commonsensical pre-training is indeed more advantageous than recognition-level pre-training. The performance increase from (e) to (f) demonstrates the effectiveness of domain-wise adaptive masking in encouraging better commonsensical multimodal learning by adaptively reducing the salience of one knowledge domain. The improvement of (g) over (f) demonstrates the effectiveness of the CTP task.

Since our high-level captions are essentially augmented captions with commonsense knowledge, we would like to see how it compares to other augmentation methods. One obvious baseline is to use a well-trained caption generator to obtain additional information for caption augmentation. We use OSCAR (Li et al., 2020), a state-of-the-art caption generator, to augment the original image caption with its generated recognition-level information. Then (c) represents the OSCAR-augmented recognition-level pre-training with Rand-1 and domain-wise adaptive masking applied. Although it improves from (b) approximately by 0.1%, it is much weaker than the increment between (b) and (f), at 0.56%. It demonstrates that the high-level commonsensical captions contain more useful and compatible information than the same amount of low-level captions do. Thus, we can conclude that the commonsense knowledge is indeed more compatible with the commonsensical reasoning ability for the downstream VCR task.

	Relevance (cap)	Relevance (img+cap)	Informativeness	Diversity
Ground Truth	3.88	3.95	3.29	3.21
Generated	3.43	3.48	3.58	3.66
Ratio	88.4%	88.0%	108.9%	114.2%

Table 4: Human evaluation of our generated commonsense inference on MSCOCO compared to the ground truth commonsense inference from VisualCOMET. "Ratio" is the score ratio of "generated" against "ground truth". The scores are on the scale of 0-5.

4.5 Commonsense Inference Evaluation

Because the MSCOCO dataset does not contain ground truth commonsense knowledge, we conduct a human evaluation on the quality of the commonsense inferences generated by our GPT-2. Following the evaluation method used in (Dua et al., 2021), we randomly sample image-caption pairs along with their corresponding generated commonsense inferences for MSCOCO and ground truth commonsense inferences from VisualCOMET, with a mixture ratio of 4:1.

We ask 10 human evaluators and have each of them evaluate 20 <image, caption, commonsense> entries without knowing whether the commonsense inferences are generated (MSCOCO) or annotated (VisualCOMET). Evaluators are asked to evaluate each commonsense inference from four dimensions on the scale of 0 to 5: *relevance (cap)*: how plausible is the commonsense inference provided the low-level caption only, *relevance (img+cap)*: how plausible is the commonsense inference given the image and the low-level caption, *informativeness*: how much extra information does the commonsense inference contain compared to the low-level caption, and *diversity*: the diversity of the five candidates commonsense inferences of each commonsense type.

We receive 12000 scores ($10 \times 20 \times 3 \times 5 \times 4$) in total. We then separate the results by generated (MSCOCO) versus annotated (VisualCOMET) and average the scores of each dimension. The results

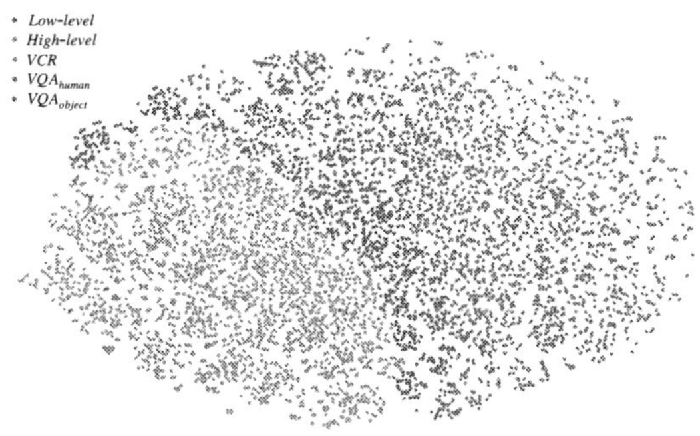

Figure 4: Corpus distribution of low-level captions, high-level captions, VCR, VQA$_{human}$, and VQA$_{object}$.

are shown in Table 4. The ground truth scores are treated as the reference for the quantified assessment of commonsense inferences quality. In terms of relevance measure, both caption-only and image-caption settings show considerable validity of our commonsense inferences on MSCOCO dataset, which is 88.4% and 88.0% of the ground truth relevance scores. It also shows that generated commonsense inferences are often more informative and diverse compared to the ground truth commonsense inferences. Detailed examples and analysis regarding the success and failure commonsense inference cases are included in Appendix A.6.

4.6 Qualitative Analysis

To understand how our proposed pre-training framework improves the downstream task performance, we perform a qualitative analysis regarding the semantic relationship among the conventional caption corpora, our pre-training corpora, and the corpora of VCR and VQA. We further separate VQA into VQA$_{human}$ and VQA$_{object}$, where VQA$_{human}$ is the human-centric VQA whose images depict human. We term VQA$_{object}$ as the object-centric VQA whose images depict things other than human. The visualization details are included in Appendix A.7. The distance between corpus distributions indicates different levels of information (e.g., recognition-level or commonsensical) and different knowledge domains (e.g., human-centric or object-centric) within each corpus.

It is easy to see that different datasets are well-separated in Figure 4. Considering the spatial relationship in the embedding space, the corpus distribution of VCR is the furthest away from that of VQA$_{object}$. This follows our intuition in that VCR and VQA$_{object}$ require different levels of understanding and reasoning and, additionally, VCR is human-centric while VQA$_{object}$ is not. The overlap between VQA$_{human}$ and VQA$_{object}$ implies that a large portion of VQA$_{human}$ is still at recognition-level. The low-level pre-training dataset also contains human-centric captions, which explains the adjacency between low-level caption corpus and VQA$_{human}$. Although the low-level caption corpus is closer to VCR than VQA is to VCR, there still exists a gap between low-level caption corpus and VCR. Our commonsensical (i.e., high-level) pre-training corpus with commonsense inferences generated by GPT-2 successfully bridges the gap between the low-level caption corpus and the downstream commonsensical corpus, which explains part of the performance improvement by our proposed method. Additionally, the distance difference between high-level caption to VQA$_{object}$ and high-level caption to VQA$_{human}$ could explain why our proposed pre-training gains larger improvement on VQA$_{human}$. It demonstrates the pre-training can generalize better to tasks with similar knowledge domains, and implies that object-centric commonsense might be more suitable for improving VQA$_{object}$.

Fine-tuning	VCR$_{sub}$ Acc. (Q→A)
VL-BERT	68.30
VL-BERT + Low-level	70.87
VL-BERT + High-level	71.17

Table 5: Fine-tuning performance comparison with additional linguistic information (without, low-level, and high-level) on the VisualCOMET subset of VCR.

4.7 Fine-tuning with High-level Captions

Besides pre-training with high-level captions, we could also introduce low-level or high-level captions as additional information to support fine-tuning on VCR. We fine-tune the VL-BERT model on a subset of VCR where the images overlap with those in VisualCOMET (VisualCOMET uses a subset of VCR images, which takes up about half the size of the full VCR.). The three settings shown in Table 5 are the original fine-tuning of VL-BERT, fine-tuning with the addition of low-level captions, and fine-tuning with the addition of high-level captions. Results show that the high-level captions are also more useful than low-level captions in helping VL-BERT improve performance during the fine-tuning stage.

5 Discussion

Summary We propose a novel visual-linguistic pre-training framework that incorporates commonsense knowledge in visual-linguistic pre-training to enhance the commonsensical reasoning ability of the model. The framework includes commonsense inference generation and two novel commonsensical pre-training tasks. The effectiveness of our pre-training framework is reflected through downstream task evaluation on VCR and VQA. We also perform extensive empirical analysis to get insights behind the improvement and demonstrate that our commonsensical pre-training is more compatible with commonsensical downstream tasks.

Limitation It is noted that the current commonsensical pre-training is bounded by the performance of the commonsensical GPT-2. Theoretically speaking, this module is replaceable by any other visual-linguistic commonsense generators or retrievers. In addition, the scope of commonsense knowledge within this work only covers the temporal and intentional domains, while the potentials of utilizing other commonsense knowledge (e.g., object-centric) in pre-training remains unexplored.

Future Work We plan to push the limits of the proposed pre-training framework by the following options: (1) Improve the quality of the existing commonsense generator; (2) Scale up the commonsensical pre-training with larger image-caption datasets, such as Conceptual Captions, and with larger vision-language models; (3) Explore more advanced commonsensical pre-training techniques other than using the extensions of the MLM objective. Another interesting direction would be exploring the pre-training effect of commonsense other than temporal and intentional knowledge.

Acknowledgement This work was supported in part by DARPA MCS program under Cooperative Agreement N66001-19-2-4032. The views expressed are those of the authors and do not reflect the official policy of the Depart- ment of Defense or the U.S. Government.

References

Stanislaw Antol, Aishwarya Agrawal, Jiasen Lu, Margaret Mitchell, Dhruv Batra, C. Lawrence Zitnick, and Devi Parikh. 2015. VQA: Visual Question Answering. In *International Conference on Computer Vision (ICCV)*.

Tom B Brown, Benjamin Mann, Nick Ryder, Melanie Subbiah, Jared Kaplan, Prafulla Dhariwal, Arvind Neelakantan, Pranav Shyam, Girish Sastry, Amanda Askell, et al. 2020. Language models are few-shot learners. *arXiv preprint arXiv:2005.14165*.

Yen-Chun Chen, Linjie Li, Licheng Yu, Ahmed El Kholy, Faisal Ahmed, Zhe Gan, Yu Cheng, and Jingjing Liu. 2020. Uniter: Universal image-text representation learning.

Jia Deng, R. Socher, Li Fei-Fei, Wei Dong, Kai Li, and Li-Jia Li. 2009. Imagenet: A large-scale hierarchical image database. In *2009 IEEE Conference on Computer Vision and Pattern Recognition(CVPR)*, volume 00, pages 248–255.

Jacob Devlin, Ming-Wei Chang, Kenton Lee, and Kristina Toutanova. 2018. Bert: Pre-training of deep bidirectional transformers for language understanding. *arXiv preprint arXiv:1810.04805*.

Radhika Dua, Sai Srinivas Kancheti, and Vineeth N. Balasubramanian. 2021. Beyond VQA: generating multi-word answers and rationales to visual questions. In *CVPR Workshops*, pages 1623–1632. Computer Vision Foundation / IEEE.

Zhe Gan, Yen-Chun Chen, Linjie Li, Chen Zhu, Yu Cheng, and Jingjing Liu. 2020. Large-scale adversarial training for vision-and-language representation learning. In *NeurIPS*.

Yash Goyal, Tejas Khot, Douglas Summers-Stay, Dhruv Batra, and Devi Parikh. 2017. Making the V in VQA matter: Elevating the role of image understanding in Visual Question Answering. In *Conference on Computer Vision and Pattern Recognition (CVPR)*.

Haoyang Huang, Yaobo Liang, Nan Duan, Ming Gong, Linjun Shou, Daxin Jiang, and Ming Zhou. 2019. Unicoder: A universal language encoder by pretraining with multiple cross-lingual tasks. In *Proceedings of the 2019 Conference on Empirical Methods in Natural Language Processing and the 9th International Joint Conference on Natural Language Processing (EMNLP-IJCNLP)*, pages 2485–2494.

Hyounghun Kim and Mohit Bansal. 2019. Improving visual question answering by referring to generated paragraph captions. In *Proceedings of the 57th Conference of the Association for Computational Linguistics, ACL 2019, Florence, Italy, July 28- August 2, 2019, Volume 1: Long Papers*, pages 3606–3612. Association for Computational Linguistics.

Ranjay Krishna, Yuke Zhu, Oliver Groth, Justin Johnson, Kenji Hata, Joshua Kravitz, Stephanie Chen, Yannis Kalantidis, Li-Jia Li, David A Shamma, Michael Bernstein, and Li Fei-Fei. 2016. Visual genome: Connecting language and vision using crowdsourced dense image annotations.

Liunian Harold Li, Mark Yatskar, Da Yin, Cho-Jui Hsieh, and Kai-Wei Chang. 2019. Visualbert: A simple and performant baseline for vision and language. *CoRR*, abs/1908.03557.

Qing Li, Jianlong Fu, Dongfei Yu, Tao Mei, and Jiebo Luo. 2018. Tell-and-answer: Towards explainable visual question answering using attributes and captions. In *EMNLP*.

Xiujun Li, Xi Yin, Chunyuan Li, Xiaowei Hu, Pengchuan Zhang, Lei Zhang, Lijuan Wang, Houdong Hu, Li Dong, Furu Wei, Yejin Choi, and Jianfeng Gao. 2020. Oscar: Object-semantics aligned pre-training for vision-language tasks. *ECCV 2020*.

Tsung-Yi Lin, Michael Maire, Serge J. Belongie, Lubomir D. Bourdev, Ross B. Girshick, James Hays, Pietro Perona, Deva Ramanan, Piotr Dollár, and C. Lawrence Zitnick. 2014. Microsoft COCO: common objects in context. *CoRR*, abs/1405.0312.

Jiasen Lu, Dhruv Batra, Devi Parikh, and Stefan Lee. 2019a. Vilbert: Pretraining task-agnostic visiolinguistic representations for vision-and-language tasks. In *Advances in Neural Information Processing Systems*, volume 32. Curran Associates, Inc.

Jiasen Lu, Dhruv Batra, Devi Parikh, and Stefan Lee. 2019b. Vilbert: Pretraining task-agnostic visiolinguistic representations for vision-and-language tasks. In *Advances in Neural Information Processing Systems*, pages 13–23.

Jae Sung Park, Chandra Bhagavatula, Roozbeh Mottaghi, Ali Farhadi, and Yejin Choi. 2020. Visualcomet: Reasoning about the dynamic context of a still image. In *In Proceedings of the European Conference on Computer Vision (ECCV)*.

Alec Radford, Karthik Narasimhan, Tim Salimans, and Ilya Sutskever. 2018. Improving language understanding by generative pre-training.

Alec Radford, Jeffrey Wu, Rewon Child, David Luan, Dario Amodei, Ilya Sutskever, et al. 2019. Language models are unsupervised multitask learners. *OpenAI blog*, 1(8):9.

Nils Reimers and Iryna Gurevych. 2020. Making monolingual sentence embeddings multilingual using knowledge distillation. In *Proceedings of the 2020 Conference on Empirical Methods in Natural Language Processing*. Association for Computational Linguistics.

Shaoqing Ren, Kaiming He, Ross B. Girshick, and Jian Sun. 2015. Faster R-CNN: towards real-time object detection with region proposal networks. *CoRR*, abs/1506.01497.

Piyush Sharma, Nan Ding, Sebastian Goodman, and Radu Soricut. 2018. Conceptual captions: A cleaned, hypernymed, image alt-text dataset for automatic image captioning. In *Proceedings of the 56th Annual Meeting of the Association for Computational Linguistics (Volume 1: Long Papers)*, pages 2556–2565.

Amanpreet Singh, Vedanuj Goswami, and Devi Parikh. 2020. Are we pretraining it right? digging deeper into visio-linguistic pretraining. *CoRR*, abs/2004.08744.

Weijie Su, Xizhou Zhu, Yue Cao, Bin Li, Lewei Lu, Furu Wei, and Jifeng Dai. 2020. Vl-bert: Pre-training of generic visual-linguistic representations. In *International Conference on Learning Representations*.

Alon Talmor, Jonathan Herzig, Nicholas Lourie, and Jonathan Berant. 2019. CommonsenseQA: A question answering challenge targeting commonsense knowledge. In *Proceedings of the 2019 Conference of the North American Chapter of the Association for Computational Linguistics: Human Language Technologies, Volume 1 (Long and Short Papers)*, pages 4149–4158, Minneapolis, Minnesota. Association for Computational Linguistics.

Hao Tan and Mohit Bansal. 2019. Lxmert: Learning cross-modality encoder representations from transformers. In *Proceedings of the 2019 Conference on Empirical Methods in Natural Language Processing*.

Ashish Vaswani, Noam Shazeer, Niki Parmar, Jakob Uszkoreit, Llion Jones, Aidan N. Gomez, Łukasz Kaiser, and Illia Polosukhin. 2017. Attention is all you need. In *Proceedings of the 31st International Conference on Neural Information Processing Systems*, NIPS'17, page 6000–6010, Red Hook, NY, USA. Curran Associates Inc.

Jialin Wu, Zeyuan Hu, and Raymond Mooney. 2019. Generating question relevant captions to aid visual question answering. In *Proceedings of the 57th Annual Meeting of the Association for Computational Linguistics*, pages 3585–3594.

Fei Yu, Jiji Tang, Weichong Yin, Yu Sun, Hao Tian, Hua Wu, and Haifeng Wang. 2020. Ernie-vil: Knowledge enhanced vision-language representations through scene graph. *CoRR*, abs/2006.16934.

Rowan Zellers, Yonatan Bisk, Ali Farhadi, and Yejin Choi. 2019. From recognition to cognition: Visual commonsense reasoning. In *The IEEE Conference on Computer Vision and Pattern Recognition (CVPR)*.

A Appendix

A.1 Transformer Revisit

The core component of Transformer (Vaswani et al., 2017) is Multi-head Self-Attention:

$$\begin{aligned}\text{MultiHead}(Q,K,V) &= \text{Concat}(\text{head}_1,...,\text{head}_h)W^O\\ \text{head}_i &= \text{Attention}(QW_i^Q, KW_i^K, VW_i^V)\\ \text{Attention}(Q,K,V) &= \text{softmax}(\frac{QK^T}{\sqrt{d_k}})V\end{aligned}$$

where the trainable weights are $W_i^Q \in \mathbb{R}^{d_{\text{model}} \times d_k}$, $W_i^K \in \mathbb{R}^{d_{\text{model}} \times d_k}$, $W_i^V \in \mathbb{R}^{d_{\text{model}} \times d_v}$ and $W^O \in \mathbb{R}^{hd_v \times d_{\text{model}}}$; d_{model}, d_k, d_v are hyperparameters and

h is the number of self-attention heads. Because it is permutation equivariant, positional encodings are injected into the token embeddings.

BERT (Devlin et al., 2018) is a deep bidirectional Transformer, which is a stack of Transformer encoder layers:

$$X = \text{MultiHead}(E^{l-1}_{out}, E^{l-1}_{out}, E^{l-1}_{out})$$
$$X' = \text{LayerNorm}(X + E^{l-1}_{out})$$
$$E^{l}_{out} = \text{LayerNorm}(\text{FFN}(X') + X')$$

where E^l_{out} are the encoder output at the lth layer. In BERT pre-training, *masked language modeling* (MLM) was proposed. It is a self-supervised setting where the model needs to predict the tokens that are masked out (with a probability of 15%) from the remaining tokens.

GPT-2 (Radford et al., 2019) is a multi-layer Transformer decoder where each decoder layer can be expressed as:

$$X = \text{MaskedMultiHead}(D^{l-1}_{out}, D^{l-1}_{out}, D^{l-1}_{out})$$
$$X' = \text{LayerNorm}(X + D^{l-1}_{out})$$
$$D^{l}_{out} = \text{LayerNorm}(\text{FFN}(X') + X')$$

where D^l_{out} are the decoder output at the lth layer.

A.2 VL-BERT Visual Features

Visual features and detected object boxes for both tasks are pre-computed and extracted by Faster R-CNN (Ren et al., 2015) that is pre-trained on the Visual-Genome (Krishna et al., 2016) dataset.

A.3 Commonsense Inference GPT-2

The GPT-2 model of VisualCOMET relies on not only the low-level captions (named "event" in VisualCOMET) but also a "place" descriptor. In order to make the model more general, we fine-tune the GPT-2 model without the "place" information: it only takes as input a pair of image and low-level caption and generates commonsense inferences, as shown in the left half of Figure 3. The visual part of the GPT-2 model is unchanged, which depends on the visual features extracted by a Faster R-CNN model.

More specifically, the input sequence is [<|b_img|>, $\mathbf{v}_0, \ldots, \mathbf{v}_m$, <|e_img|>, <|b_ev|>, $\mathbf{l}_0, \ldots, \mathbf{l}_n$, <|e_ev|>, <|before|>], where $\mathbf{v}$ and $\mathbf{l}$ are visual features and word embeddings, respectively; <|b_⋯|> and <|e_⋯|> are special tokens for marking the beginning and the end of the image and "event" sequences; the <|before|> token can also be replaced with <|after|> or <|intent|> to specify what type of commonsense inference to generate.

A.4 High-level Caption Construction

After the three types of commonsense inferences are generated by GPT-2 for each image, we construct high-level captions by merging the original (low-level) caption with commonsense inference using the following templates:

- Before [low], [person] wanted to [commonsense inference].
- After [low], [person] will most likely [commonsense inference].
- Because [person] wanted to [commonsense inference], [low].

where [person] is the extracted subject name, [low] is the low-level caption and [commonsense inference] is the generated type-specific commonsense inference; all other tokens are named *template tokens* (e.g., Before ... wanted to). The "Inference section" of Figure 3 includes an example of such high-level caption.

We take the MSCOCO dataset (Lin et al., 2014) as our base pre-training dataset. It contains 533K unique image-caption pairs. Since VCR is a human-centric reasoning task, we filter MSCOCO by keyword matching with an pre-defined person-entity vocabulary (e.g., student, firefighter) and obtain its human-centric subset. We then generate human-centric commonsense inference on it. Our final pre-training dataset contains 257K unique low-level image-caption pairs and 3915K ($\approx 3\times 5\times 257$K) unique high-level image-caption pairs.

A.5 Domain-wise Adaptive Masking Computation

The *domain-wise adaptive masking* ratio is computed by the equations below:

$$score = \text{cos\_sim}(\mathbf{h}_{low}, \mathbf{h}_{CI})$$
$$ratio = \text{Rescale}(\sigma(score)))$$

where $\mathbf{h}_{low}$ is the sentence embedding for the low-level captions, and $\mathbf{h}_{CI}$ is the sentence embedding for its corresponding commonsense inferences. The sentence representation is the representation of the [CLS] token taken from BERT; $cos\_sim(\cdot)$ is the cosine similarity; $\sigma(\cdot)$ is the logistic function; Rescale is the min-max scaling, where the prior minimum and prior maximum are precomputed from the training data. In this work, the posterior range is $(0.5, 1)$. Figure 5 is the histogram of the computed adaptive masking ratios from the training data with the mean ratio equals to 0.715. Examples of the calculated masking ratio are shown in Figure 6. Since "stop skiing" is more semantically related to "middle of a skiing jump", the function outputs a larger masking ratio compared to "fear for his life". The same idea follows as the "get served piazza" is more semantically related to "in front of two piazzas" compared to "gather the ingredients".

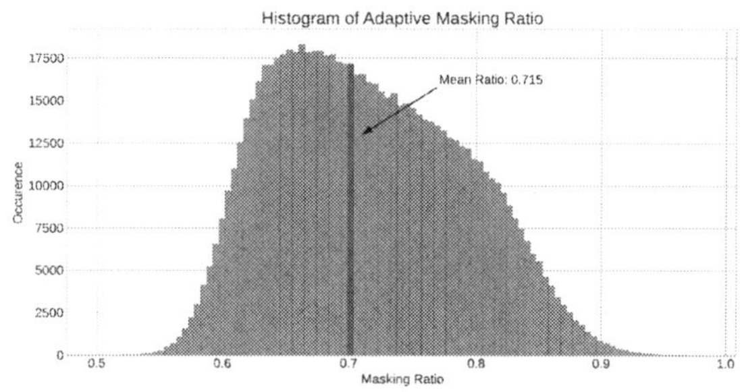

Figure 5: Histogram of the adaptive masking ratio from the training data.

A.6 Commonsense Inference Evaluation

The generated commonsense inferences on MSCOCO are evaluated by human annotators from four dimensions on the scale of 0-5: relevant score given the caption only, relevant score given the image-caption pair, informative level, and diversity level. We include two examples in Figure 7, which corresponds to the success case and the failure case of the commonsense inference considering the evaluation scores. In the success case (Figure 7a), even though the caption mistakenly treats the Frisbee as a white ball, our commonsense inference GPT-2 successfully identifies the Frisbee and generates the commonsense inferences accordingly. The noisy caption explains the low scores in rel_1. The high rel_2 scores show the strength of our commonsense generator. Commonsense inferences in Figure 7b are evaluated as poorly generated. Both of its rel_1 and rel_2 scores are much lower. Compared to its image with the success case, we can see that it depicts a much larger scene where object details are harder to be perceived by the model. For example, the skier is doing tricks, while it can be ambiguous for the model to even identify human-alike shapes. However, the GPT-2 seems to recognize the scene as a big event. On the other hand, we can see that high information-level can be due to either inadequate captions, valid and informative commonsense inferences, or noisy commonsense inferences. The examples also show how the diversity-level can be positively correlated with the ambiguity-level of the images and negatively correlated with the relevant scores. It introduces some insights behind the higher informative and diversity score of the generated commonsense inferences in Table 4.

A.7 Corpora Visualization

We randomly sample 10K "sentences" from each dataset to estimate their corpus distribution. For low-level pre-training and commonsensical pre-training, sentences simply refer to the low-level captions and high-level captions, respectively. For VQA, a sentence is the concatenation of a question and its corresponding ground truth answer with the highest confidence. The VQA corpus is further divided into human-centric VQA and object-oriented VQA. In VCR, a sentence is the concatenation of a question, its corresponding answer, and the ground truth rationale.

We use a pre-trained Sentence-BERT (Reimers and Gurevych, 2020) to retrieve the embedding of each sentence. Then each of the five datasets is represented by an embedding matrix of size $10,000 \times 768$, where 10,000 is the sample size and 768 is the hidden dimension size. We use the t-SNE nonlinear dimension reduction technique to project and plot the corpus distributions in a 2-dimensional space, as shown in Figure 4.

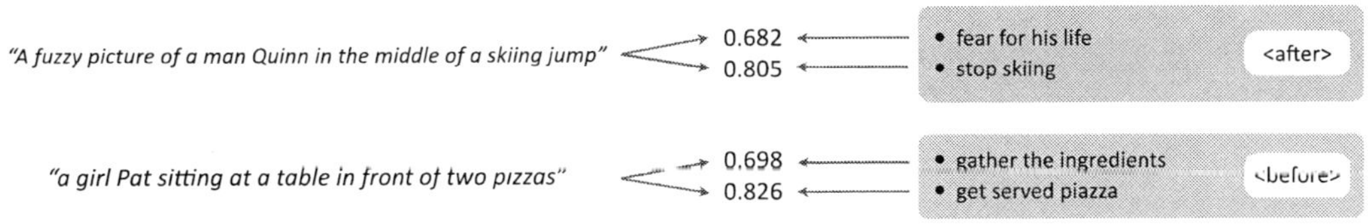

Figure 6: Examples of the calculated domain-wise adaptive masking ratio from low-level captions (left) and commonsense inferences (right).

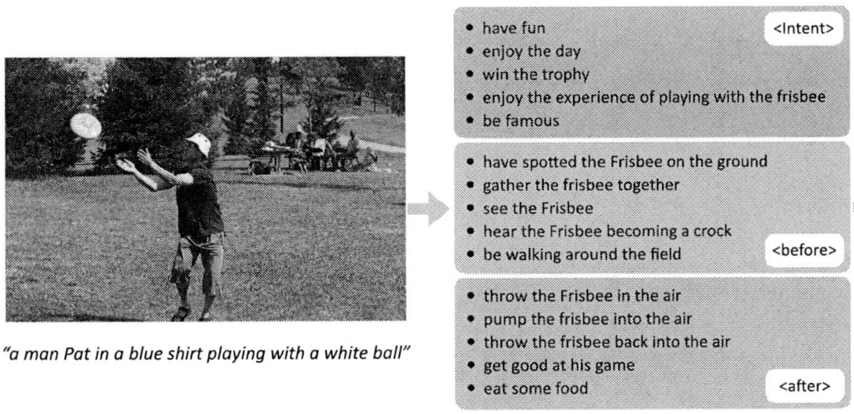

rel_1	rel_2	*info*	*div*
4	5	3	3
4	5	3	3
2	2	5	5
2	5	3	3
3	3	5	5
1	5	5	4
1	5	5	4
1	5	5	4
0	0	5	5
3	2	5	5
1	5	5	2
1	5	5	3
1	5	4	2
1	4	4	4
5	5	3	3

(a) Success Case

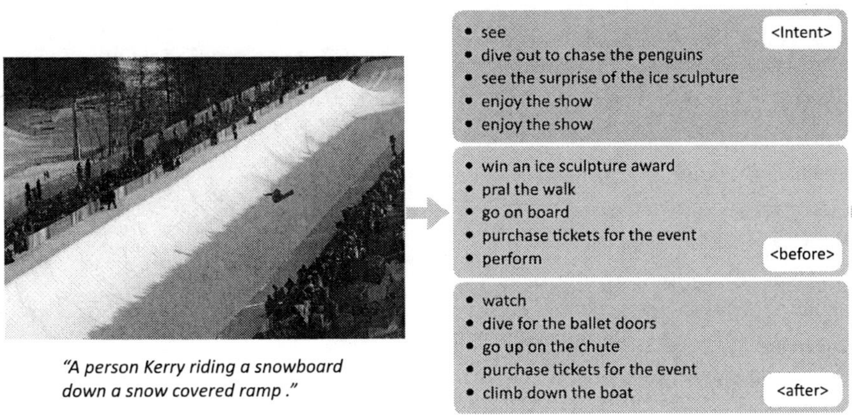

rel_1	rel_2	*info*	*div*
2	3	5	4
4	0	3	3
2	1	5	3
4	3	5	3
3	3	5	3
3	0	5	3
3	1	5	5
0	3	4	5
5	2	2	5
3	4	5	5
2	4	3	5
4	1	3	5
1	5	5	5
1	2	5	5
1	0	5	5

(b) Failure Case

Figure 7: Examples of generated commonsense inference on MSCOCO with human evaluation. Left: image-caption pair as the inputs of the commonsense generator; Middle: generated commonsense inference; Right: human evaluation from four dimensions: rel_1 is the relevant score given the caption only; rel_2 is the relevant score given the image-caption pair; $info$ is the informative score; div is the diversity score.

Materialized Knowledge Bases from Commonsense Transformers

Tuan-Phong Nguyen
Max Planck Institute for Informatics
Saarland Informatics Campus
Saarbrücken, Germany
tuanphong@mpi-inf.mpg.de

Simon Razniewski
Max Planck Institute for Informatics
Saarland Informatics Campus
Saarbrücken, Germany
srazniew@mpi-inf.mpg.de

Abstract

Starting from the COMET methodology by Bosselut et al. (2019), generating commonsense knowledge from commonsense transformers has recently received significant attention. Surprisingly, up to now no materialized resource of commonsense knowledge generated this way is publicly available. This paper fills this gap, and uses the materialized resources to perform a detailed analysis of the potential of this approach in terms of precision and recall. Furthermore, we identify common problem cases, and outline use cases enabled by materialized resources. We posit that the availability of these resources is important for the advancement of the field, as it enables an off-the-shelf-use of the resulting knowledge, as well as further analyses on its strengths and weaknesses.

1 Introduction

Compiling comprehensive collections of commonsense knowledge (CSK) is an old dream of AI. Besides attempts at manual compilation (Liu and Singh, 2004; Lenat, 1995; Sap et al., 2018) and text extraction (Schubert, 2002; Tandon et al., 2014; Mishra et al., 2017; Romero et al., 2019; Nguyen et al., 2021a), commonsense knowledge compilation from pretrained language models (Bosselut et al., 2019; Hwang et al., 2021; West et al., 2021) has recently emerged. In 2019, Bosselut et al. introduced *Commonsense Transformers* (COMET), an approach for fine-tuning language models on existing corpora of commonsense assertions. These models have shown promising performance in generating commonsense assertions after being trained on established human-authored commonsense resources such as ATOMIC (Sap et al., 2018) and ATOMIC$^{20}_{20}$ (Hwang et al., 2021).

More recently, West et al. (2021) extracts commonsense assertions from a general language model, GPT-3 (Brown et al., 2020), using simple prompting techniques. Surprisingly, using this machine-authored commonsense corpus to fine-tune COMET helps it outperform GPT-3, which is 100x larger in size, in terms of commonsense capabilities.

Despite the prominence of this approach (the seminal COMET paper (Bosselut et al., 2019) receiving over 300 citations in just two years), to date, no resource containing commonsense knowledge compiled from any COMET model is publicly available. As compilation of such a resource is a non-trivial endeavour, this is a major impediment to research that aims to understand the potentials of the approach, or intends to employ its outputs in downstream tasks.

This resource paper fills this gap. We fine-tune the COMET pipeline on two established resources of concept-centric CSK assertions, CONCEPTNET (Speer et al., 2017) and ASCENT++ (Nguyen et al., 2021a), and execute the pipeline for 10K prominent subjects. Unlike the ATOMIC resources, which were used to train COMET in (Bosselut et al., 2019; Hwang et al., 2021) and have their main focus on events and social interactions, the two resources of choice are mostly about general concepts (e.g., *lions can roar*, or *a car has four wheels*). Furthermore, as those two resources were constructed using two fundamentally different methods, crowdsourcing and web text extraction, it enables us to discover potentially different impacts they have on the COMET models.

By taking the top-10 inferences for each subject-predicate pair, we obtain four resources, CONCEPTNET (GPT2-XL, BART) and ASCENT++ (GPT2-XL, BART), containing 900K to 1.4M ranked assertions of CSK. We perform a detailed evaluation of the intrinsic quality, including fine-grained precision (typicality and saliency) and recall of each resource, derive qualitative insights into the strengths and weaknesses of the approach, and highlight extrinsic use cases enabled by the resources.

Proceedings of the First Workshop on Commonsense Representation and Reasoning (CSRR 2021), pages 36 - 42
May 27, 2022

Our contributions are:

1. The materialization of the COMET approach for two language models (GPT2-XL, BART) on two concept-centered commonsense knowledge bases (CONCEPTNET, ASCENT++);

2. Quantitative and qualitative evaluations of the resulting resources in terms of precision, recall and error categories, showing that in terms of recall, COMET models outperform crowdsourced construction and are competitive with web text extraction, while exhibiting moderate gaps in terms of precision to both;

3. Illustrative use cases of the materialized resources in statement aggregation, join queries, and search.

The materialized resources, as well as an interactive browsing interface, are available at `https://ascentpp.mpi-inf.mpg.de/comet`.

2 Related work

Early approaches at CSK compilation relied on expert knowledge engineers (Lenat, 1995) or crowdsourcing (Liu and Singh, 2004), and the latter approach has recently been revived (Sap et al., 2018). To overcome scalability limitations of manual compilation, text extraction is a second popular paradigm. Following early attempts on linguistic corpora (Mishra et al., 2017), increasingly approaches have targeted larger text corpora like Wikipedia, book scans, or web documents (Tandon et al., 2014; Romero et al., 2019; Nguyen et al., 2021a,b), to build CSK resources of wide coverage and quality.

Recently, both approaches have been complemented by knowledge extraction from pretrained language models: Language models like BERT (Devlin et al., 2019) or GPT (Radford et al., 2019; Brown et al., 2020) have seen millions of documents, and latently store associations among terms. While West et al. (2021) used prompting to extract symbolic CSK from GPT-3, Bosselut et al. (2019) proposed to tap this knowledge by supervised learning: The language models are fine-tuned on statements from existing knowledge resources, e.g., trained to predict the object *Africa* when given the subject-predicate pair *elephant, AtLocation*, based on the ConceptNet triple ⟨*elephant, AtLocation, Africa*⟩. After training, they can be used to predict objects for unseen subject-predicate pairs, e.g., locations of wombats.

The approach gained significant attention, and variants are employed in a range of downstream tasks, e.g., commonsense question answering (Bosselut and Choi, 2020), commonsense explanation (Wang et al., 2020), story generation (Guan et al., 2020), or video captioning (Fang et al., 2020).

Yet, to date, no materialized knowledge resource produced by any COMET model is available (AUTOTOMIC from (West et al., 2021) being based on prompting GPT-3). The closest to this is a web interface hosted by the AllenAI institute at `https://mosaickg.apps.allenai.org/model_comet2020_entities`. However, this visualizes only predictions for a single subject, making, e.g., aggregations or count impossible, and only shows top-5 predictions, and without scores.

3 Methodology

We follow the implementations in the official code repository[1] of the COMET-ATOMIC$^{20}_{20}$ project (Hwang et al., 2021) to compute assertions, and decide on output thresholds.

Training CSKBs. We use two established concept-centered commonsense knowledge bases (CSKBs), CONCEPTNET 5.7 (Speer et al., 2017) and ASCENT++ (Nguyen et al., 2021a) as training resources, considering 13 CSK predicates from each of them: *AtLocation*, *CapableOf*, *Causes*, *Desires*, *HasA*, *HasPrerequisite*, *HasProperty*, *HasSubevent*, *MadeOf*, *MotivatedByGoal*, *PartOf*, *UsedFor* and *ReceivesAction*.

1. CONCEPTNET (Speer et al., 2017) is arguably the most widely used CSKB, built by crowdsourcing. CONCEPTNET 5.7 is its lastest version[2], consisting of 21 million multilingual assertions, spanning CSK as well as general linguistic and taxonomic knowledge. We retain English assertions only, resulting in 207,210 training assertions for the above-mentioned predicates.

2. ASCENT++ (Nguyen et al., 2021a) is a project aiming for automated CSK extraction from large-scaled web contents based on open information extraction (OpenIE) and judicious

[1] `https://github.com/allenai/comet-atomic-2020/`

[2] `https://github.com/commonsense/conceptnet5/wiki/Downloads`

Parameter	GPT2-XL	BART
num_beams	10	10
temperature	1.0	1.0
top_p	0.9	1.0
repetition_penalty	1.0	1.0
max_length	16	24
no_repeat_ngram_size	0	3
early_stopping	True	True
do_sample	False	False

Table 1: Configurations for beam-search decoders.

cleaning and ranking approaches. The ASCENT++ KB consists of 2 million English CSK assertions for the 13 mentioned predicates.

Language models. We consider two autoregressive language models (LMs) that were also used in the original COMET paper, GPT2-XL (Radford et al., 2019) and BART (Lewis et al., 2020).

Materialization process. We query the fine-tuned COMET models for 10,926 subjects in CONCEPTNET which have at least two assertions for the 13 CSK predicates. For each subject-predicate pair, we use beam search to obtain completions, with different configurations (see Table 1) for BART and GPT2-XL, following the parameters specified in the published code repository and models. We retain the top-10 completions for each subject-predicate pair, with their *beam scores* (i.e., sum of log softmax of all generated tokens) returned by the *generate* function[3] of the Transformers library (Wolf et al., 2020).

Output. The resulting resources, CONCEPTNET (GPT2-XL, BART) and ASCENT++ (GPT2-XL, BART), contain a total of 976,296 and 1,420,380 and 1,271,295 and 1,420,380 assertions after deduplication, respectively, as well as their corresponding beam scores. All are available for browsing, as well as for download, at `https://ascentpp.mpi-inf.mpg.de/comet` (see screenshot of browsing interface in Figure 2).

4 Analysis

We perform three kind of analyses: (1) a quantitative evaluation of the intrinsic quality of the assertions, based on crowdsourcing, (2) a qualitative evaluation that outlines major strengths and weaknesses, and (3) an illustration of use cases enabled by both resources.

4.1 Quantitative evaluation

The original paper (Bosselut et al., 2019) only evaluated the top-1 triple per subject-predicate pair. Furthermore, it solely evaluated triples by plausibility, which is a necessary, but only partly a sufficient criterion for being considered commonsense (Chalier et al., 2020).

In the following, we evaluate samples from the generated resources along two *precision* dimensions, typicality (top-100 assertions per subject) and saliency (top-10 assertions per subject). We also evaluate *recall*, by measuring the degree to which each resource covers the statements in a human-generated ground truth.

Precision: Typicality and saliency. Following Romero et al. (2019); Nguyen et al. (2021a), we assess assertions in the CSK resources along two precision dimensions: *typicality* and *saliency*, which measure the degree of truth and the degree of relevance of assertions, respectively. We use the Amazon Mechanical Turk (AMT) platform to obtain human judgements. Each dimension is evaluated based on a 4-point Likert scale and an option for *no judgement* if the annotator is not familiar with the concepts. Assertions are transformed into human-readable sentences using the templates introduced by Hwang et al. (2021). Each assignment is done by three different workers. Following Hwang et al. (2021), any CSK assertion that receives the two higher scores in the Likert scale is labelled as *Typical* or *Salient*, and the two lower scores as *Untypical* or *Unsalient*. The final judgements is based on majority vote.

In terms of sampling process, for typicality, we draw 500 assertions from each resource when restricting to top-100 assertions per subject. For saliency, we pick 500 random samples from the pool of top-10 assertions per subject.

Results are reported in the left part of Table 2. We see a significant drop in the quality of assertions in the LM-based generations compared to the training resources. In terms of the neural models, for both training CSKBs, the BART models demonstrate better typicality than the GPT2-XL ones. Assertions in BART-ASCENT++ also have significantly better saliency than in GPT2-XL-ASCENT++. Interestingly, BART-CONCEPTNET

[3] `https://huggingface.co/docs/transformers/main/en/main_classes/text_generation#transformers.generation_utils.GenerationMixin.generate`

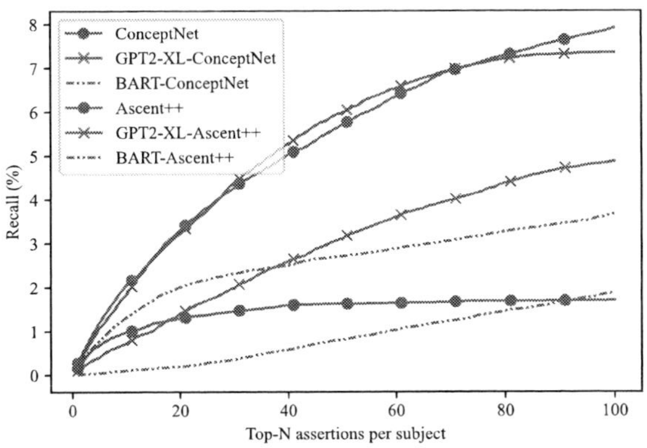

Figure 1: Resource recall in relation to resource size, at similarity threshold $t = 0.98$.

is nearly on par with ASCENT++ on both metrics.

Recall. We reuse the CSLB dataset (Devereux et al., 2014) that was processed by Nguyen et al. (2021a) as ground truth for recall evaluation. The CSLB dataset consists of 22.6K human-written sentences about property norms of 638 concepts. To account for minor reformulations, following Nguyen et al. (2021a), we also use embedding-based similarity to match ground-truth sentences with statements in the CSK resources. We specifically rely on precomputed SentenceTransformers embeddings (Reimers and Gurevych, 2019). We also restrict all CSK resources to top-100 assertions per subject.

The evaluation results are shown in the right part of Table 2, where we report recall at similarity thresholds 0.96, 0.98 and 1.0, as well as resource size. We also plot the recall values at different top-N assertions per subject in Figure 1 with similarity threshold $t = 0.98$. As one can see, ASCENT++ outperforms both COMET models trained on it even though it is significantly smaller. We see opposite results with the CONCEPTNET-based resources, where the COMET models generate resources of better coverage than its training data. Our presumption is that the LMs profits more from manually curated resources like CONCEPTNET, but hardly add values to resources that were extracted from the web, as LMs have not seen fundamentally different text. Furthermore, in contrast to precision, GPT2-XL models have better results than BART models in terms of recall, on both input CSKBs.

4.2 Qualitative observations

LMs have the strength to generate an open-ended set of objects, even for subjects seen rarely or not at all in the training data. For example, while CONCEPTNET stores only one location for *rabbit*: *"a meadow"*, both BART- and GPT2-XL-CONCEPTNET can generalize to other correct locations, such as *wilderness, zoo, cage, pet store*, etc. In the recall evaluation, we pointed out that CONCEPTNET, a manually-built CSK resource with relatively small size, considerably benefits from LMs generations as they improve the coverage of the resource substantially.

However, as indicated in the precision evaluation, LM generations are generally of lower precision than those in the training data. Common error categories we observe are:

- **Co-occurrence misreadings:** LMs frequently predict values that merely frequently co-occur, e.g., ⟨*locomotive, atLocation, bus stop*⟩, ⟨*running, capableOf, put on shoes*⟩, ⟨*war, desires, kill people*⟩, ⟨*supermarket, capableOf, buy milk*⟩.
- **Subject-object-copying**: LMs too often repeat the given subject in predictions. For instance, 45 of 130 objects generated by BART-CONCEPTNET for the subject *chicken* also contain *chicken*, such as ⟨*chicken, CapableOf, kill/eat/cook chicken*⟩ or ⟨*chicken, UsedFor, feed chicken*⟩.
- **Quantity confusion**: LMs struggle to distinguish quantities. For example, GPT2-XL-CONCEPTNET generates that *bike* has *four wheels* (top-1 prediction), and then also *two wheels* (rank 3), *three wheels* (rank 4) and *twelve wheels* (rank 5). The weakness of dealing with numbers is known as a common issue of embeddings-based approaches (Berg-Kirkpatrick and Spokoyny, 2020).
- **Redundancy**: Generated objects often overlap, bloating the output with redundancies. Most common are repetitions of singular/plural nouns, e.g., the top-2 generations by BART-CONCEPTNET for *doctor-CapableOf*: *"visit patient"* and *"visit patients"*. Redundancies also include paraphrases, e.g., ⟨*doctor, CapableOf, visit patients / see patients*⟩; or ⟨*doctor, CapableOf, prescribe medication / prescribe drug / prescribe medicine*⟩ (GPT2-XL-ASCENT++ generations). Clustering might alleviate this issue (Nguyen et al., 2021a).

Resource	Typicality@100		Saliency@10		Recall@100			Size@100
	Typical	Untypical	Salient	Unsalient	t=0.96	t=0.98	t=1.00	#triples
ASCENT++	**78.4**	**11.0**	**62.8**	**34.6**	**8.9**	**7.9**	**4.6**	202,026
GPT2-XL-ASCENT++	57.2	27.4	37.2	58.4	6.0	4.9	2.6	1,091,662
BART-ASCENT++	69.8	17.4	50.6	42.6	2.6	1.9	1.0	1,092,600
CONCEPTNET	**93.6**	**3.6**	**80.0**	**16.8**	2.3	1.7	0.9	164,291
GPT2-XL-CONCEPTNET	66.6	21.4	63.8	32.6	**9.0**	**7.3**	**3.8**	967,343
BART-CONCEPTNET	72.6	17.0	63.4	33.4	5.3	3.7	1.0	1,092,600

Table 2: Intrinsic evaluation (Typicality, Saliency and Recall - %) and size of CSK resources.

4.3 Downstream use of materialized resources

Beyond systematic evaluation, materialized resources enable a wide set of downstream use cases, for example context-enriched zero-shot question answering (Petroni et al., 2020), or KB-based commonsense explanation (Wang et al., 2020). We exemplarily illustrate four enabled types of basic analyses, (1) frequency aggregation, (2) join queries, (3) ranking and (4) text search.

Frequency aggregation. Materialized resources enable to count frequencies. In Table 3, we demonstrate the three most common objects for each predicate in the GPT2-XL-CONCEPTNET resource. Interestingly, the third most common location of items in the KB is *"sock drawer"*, which is only ranked as the 190th most common location in CONCEPTNET. Similarly, the top-3 objects for *CapableOf* in the generated KB rarely occur the training data.

Predicate	Most common objects
AtLocation	desk (3210), cabinet (2481), sock drawer (1771)
CapableOf	branch out (963), branch off (747), taste good (556)
Causes	death (2504), tears (1290), happiness (1254)
Desires	eat (949), have fun (816), sex (742)
HasA	more than one meaning (1387), seeds (1316), peel (1170)
HasPrerequisite	metal (1965), plastic (1594), water (1423)
HasProperty	good (2615), useful (2585), good for (1746)
HasSubevent	breathe (1006), swallow (721), take off shoes (658)
MadeOf	plastic (1427), aluminum (1297), wood (905)
MotivatedByGoal	have fun (994), enjoyment (493), succeed (444)
PartOf	new testament (914), human experience (683), alabama (667)
ReceivesAction	found in house (1110), eaten (800), found in hospital (779)
UsedFor	cooking (627), decoration (454), transport (448)

Table 3: Most common objects generated by GPT2-XL-CONCEPTNET. Numbers in parentheses indicate frequency of the corresponding objects.

Join queries. One level further, materialized knowledge enables the construction of join queries. For example, we can formulate conjunctive queries like:

- Animals that eat themselves include *chicken, flies, grasshopper, mice, penguin, worm.*
- The most frequent subevents of subevents are: *breathe, swallow, hold breath, think, smile.*
- The most common parts of locations are: *beaches, seeds, lot of trees, peel, more than one meaning.*

Ranking. Since statements in our materialized resources come with scores, it becomes possible to locally and globally rank assertions, or to compare statements pairwise. For example, in GPT2-XL-CONCEPTNET, the triple ⟨*librarian, AtLocation, library*⟩, which is at rank 140, has a score of -0.048, which is much higher than that of ⟨*elephant, CapableOf, climb tree*⟩ (score = -0.839, ranked 638,048 globally).

Text search. Finally, we can use materialized resources for text search. For example, we can search in GPT2-XL-CONCEPTNET for all assertions that include the term *"airplane"*, finding expected matches like ⟨*airplane, AtLocation, airport*⟩ and ⟨*flight attendant, CapableOf, travel on airplane*⟩, as well as surprising ones like ⟨*scrap paper, UsedFor, making paper airplane*⟩ and ⟨*traveling, HasSubevent, sleeping on airplane*⟩.

5 Conclusion

We introduced four CSKBs computed using two COMET models (BART and GPT2-XL) trained on two existing CSK resources (CONCEPTNET and ASCENT++). Our findings are:

1. The COMET methodology produces better results on modest manually curated resources (CONCEPTNET) than on larger web-extracted resources (ASCENT++).

2. COMET's recall can significantly outperform that of modest manually curated ones (CONCEPTNET), and reach that of large web-extracted ones (ASCENT++).

3. In terms of precision, a significant gap remains to manual curation, both in typicality and saliency. To web extraction, a moderate gap remains in terms of statement typicality.

We also identified common problems of the COMET generations, such as co-occurrence misreadings, subject copying, and redundancies, which may be subject of further research regarding post-filtering and clustering.

References

Taylor Berg-Kirkpatrick and Daniel Spokoyny. 2020. An empirical investigation of contextualized number prediction. In *EMNLP*.

Antoine Bosselut and Yejin Choi. 2020. Dynamic knowledge graph construction for zero-shot commonsense question answering. In *AAAI*.

Antoine Bosselut, Hannah Rashkin, Maarten Sap, Chaitanya Malaviya, Asli Çelikyilmaz, and Yejin Choi. 2019. COMET: commonsense transformers for automatic knowledge graph construction. In *ACL*.

Tom B. Brown et al. 2020. Language models are few-shot learners. In *NeurIPS*.

Yohan Chalier, Simon Razniewski, and Gerhard Weikum. 2020. Joint reasoning for multi-faceted commonsense knowledge. In *AKBC*.

Barry J Devereux, Lorraine K Tyler, Jeroen Geertzen, and Billi Randall. 2014. The centre for speech, language and the brain (CSLB) concept property norms. *Behavior research methods*.

Jacob Devlin, Ming-Wei Chang, Kenton Lee, and Kristina Toutanova. 2019. Bert: Pre-training of deep bidirectional transformers for language understanding. In *NAACL*.

Zhiyuan Fang, Tejas Gokhale, Pratyay Banerjee, Chitta Baral, and Yezhou Yang. 2020. Video2commonsense: Generating commonsense descriptions to enrich video captioning. In *EMNLP*.

Jian Guan, Fei Huang, Zhihao Zhao, Xiaoyan Zhu, and Minlie Huang. 2020. A knowledge-enhanced pretraining model for commonsense story generation. *TACL*.

Jena D. Hwang, Chandra Bhagavatula, Ronan Le Bras, Jeff Da, Keisuke Sakaguchi, Antoine Bosselut, and Yejin Choi. 2021. (Comet-)Atomic 2020: On symbolic and neural commonsense knowledge graphs. In *AAAI*.

Douglas B Lenat. 1995. Cyc: A large-scale investment in knowledge infrastructure. *CACM*.

Mike Lewis, Yinhan Liu, Naman Goyal, Marjan Ghazvininejad, Abdelrahman Mohamed, Omer Levy, Ves Stoyanov, and Luke Zettlemoyer. 2020. Bart: Denoising sequence-to-sequence pre-training for natural language generation, translation, and comprehension. In *ACL*.

Hugo Liu and Push Singh. 2004. Conceptnet—a practical commonsense reasoning tool-kit. *BT technology journal*.

Bhavana Dalvi Mishra, Niket Tandon, and Peter Clark. 2017. Domain-targeted, high precision knowledge extraction. *TACL*.

Tuan-Phong Nguyen, Simon Razniewski, Julien Romero, and Gerhard Weikum. 2021a. Refined commonsense knowledge from large-scale web contents. *arXiv preprint arXiv:2112.04596*.

Tuan-Phong Nguyen, Simon Razniewski, and Gerhard Weikum. 2021b. Advanced semantics for commonsense knowledge extraction. In *WWW*.

Fabio Petroni, Patrick Lewis, Aleksandra Piktus, Tim Rocktäschel, Yuxiang Wu, Alexander H Miller, and Sebastian Riedel. 2020. How context affects language models' factual predictions. In *AKBC*.

Alec Radford, Jeffrey Wu, Rewon Child, David Luan, Dario Amodei, Ilya Sutskever, et al. 2019. Language models are unsupervised multitask learners. *OpenAI blog*, 1(8):9.

Nils Reimers and Iryna Gurevych. 2019. Sentence-bert: Sentence embeddings using siamese bert-networks. In *EMNLP*.

Julien Romero, Simon Razniewski, Koninika Pal, Jeff Z. Pan, Archit Sakhadeo, and Gerhard Weikum. 2019. Commonsense properties from query logs and question answering forums. In *CIKM*.

Maarten Sap, Ronan LeBras, Emily Allaway, Chandra Bhagavatula, Nicholas Lourie, Hannah Rashkin, Brendan Roof, Noah A Smith, and Yejin Choi. 2018. Atomic: An atlas of machine commonsense for if-then reasoning. In *AAAI*.

Lenhart Schubert. 2002. Can we derive general world knowledge from texts. In *HLT*.

Robyn Speer, Joshua Chin, and Catherine Havasi. 2017. Conceptnet 5.5: An open multilingual graph of general knowledge. In *AAAI*.

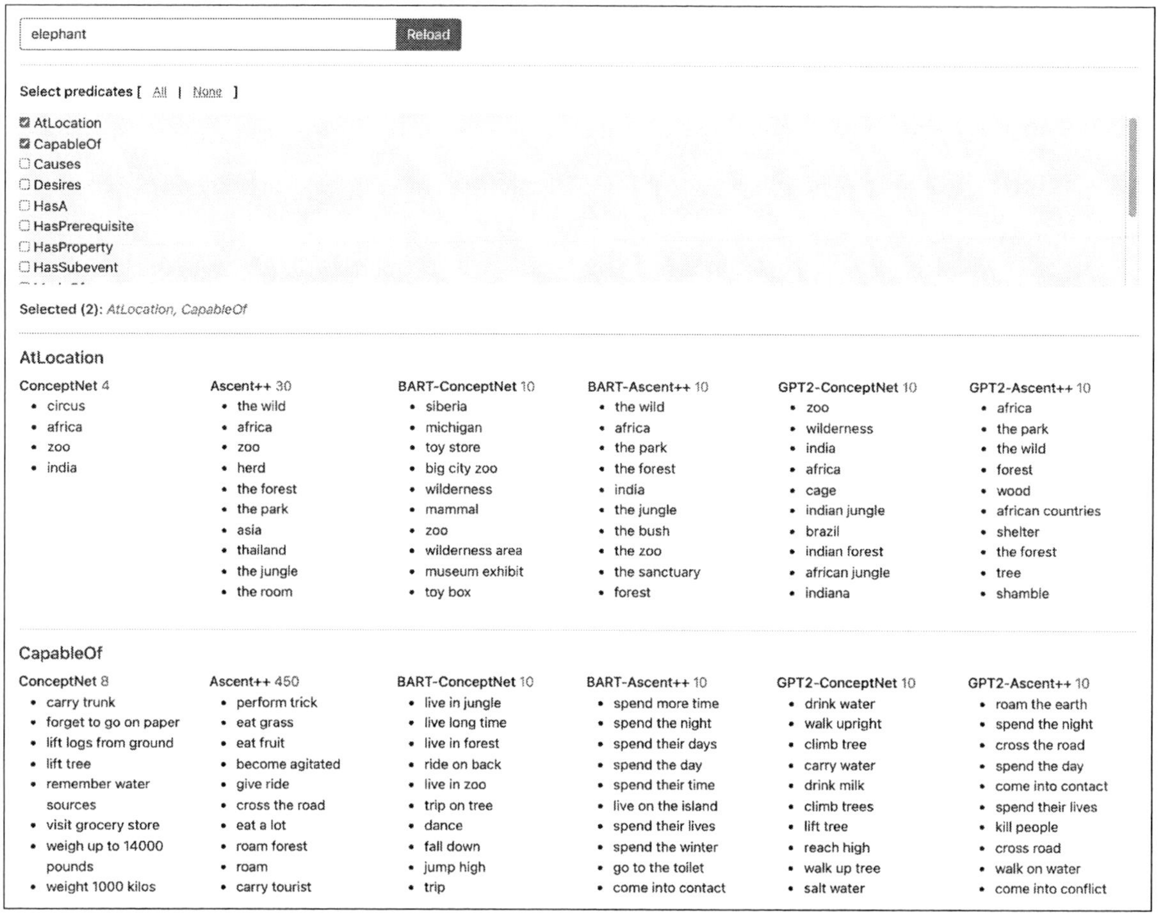

Figure 2: Web interface showing top-10 assertions per predicate in six CSK resources. The number in grey next to a CSKB indicates the total number of assertions for the corresponding subject-predicate pair in the KB.

Niket Tandon, Gerard de Melo, Fabian M. Suchanek, and Gerhard Weikum. 2014. WebChild: harvesting and organizing commonsense knowledge from the web. In *WSDM*.

Cunxiang Wang, Shuailong Liang, Yili Jin, Yilong Wang, Xiaodan Zhu, and Yue Zhang. 2020. Semeval-2020 task 4: Commonsense validation and explanation. In *SemEval*.

Peter West, Chandra Bhagavatula, Jack Hessel, Jena D Hwang, Liwei Jiang, Ronan Le Bras, Ximing Lu, Sean Welleck, and Yejin Choi. 2021. Symbolic knowledge distillation: from general language models to commonsense models. *arXiv preprint arXiv:2110.07178*.

Thomas Wolf, Lysandre Debut, Victor Sanh, Julien Chaumond, Clement Delangue, Anthony Moi, Pierric Cistac, Tim Rault, Remi Louf, Morgan Funtowicz, Joe Davison, Sam Shleifer, Patrick von Platen, Clara Ma, Yacine Jernite, Julien Plu, Canwen Xu, Teven Le Scao, Sylvain Gugger, Mariama Drame, Quentin Lhoest, and Alexander Rush. 2020. Transformers: State-of-the-art natural language processing. In *EMLNP: System Demonstrations*.

Knowledge-Augmented Language Models for Cause-Effect Relation Classification

Pedram Hosseini[1] **David A. Broniatowski**[1] **Mona Diab**[1,2]
[1]The George Washington University [2]Meta AI
phosseini@gwu.edu

Abstract

Previous studies have shown the efficacy of knowledge augmentation methods in pretrained language models. However, these methods behave differently across domains and downstream tasks. In this work, we investigate the augmentation of pretrained language models with knowledge graph data in the cause-effect relation classification and commonsense causal reasoning tasks. After automatically verbalizing triples in ATOMIC$^{20}_{20}$, a wide coverage commonsense reasoning knowledge graph, we continually pretrain BERT and evaluate the resulting model on cause-effect pair classification and answering commonsense causal reasoning questions. Our results show that a continually pretrained language model augmented with commonsense reasoning knowledge outperforms our baselines on two commonsense causal reasoning benchmarks, COPA and BCOPA-CE, and a Temporal and Causal Reasoning (TCR) dataset, without additional improvement in model architecture or using quality-enhanced data for fine-tuning.

1 Introduction

Automatic extraction and classification of causal relations in text has been an important yet challenging task in natural language understanding. Early methods in the 80s and 90s (Joskowicz et al., 1989; Kaplan and Berry-Rogghe, 1991; Garcia et al., 1997; Khoo et al., 1998) mainly relied on defining hand-crafted rules to find cause-effect relations. Starting 2000, machine learning tools were utilized in building causal relation extraction models (Girju, 2003; Chang and Choi, 2004, 2006; Blanco et al., 2008; Do et al., 2011; Hashimoto et al., 2012; Hidey and McKeown, 2016). Word-embeddings and Pretrained Language Models (PLMs) have also been leveraged in training models for understanding causality in language in recent years (Dunietz et al., 2018; Pennington et al., 2014; Dasgupta et al., 2018; Gao et al., 2019).

Investigating the true capability of pretrained language models in understanding causality in text is still an open question. More recently, Knowledge Graphs (KGs) have been used in combination with pretrained language models to address commonsense reasoning. Two examples are CausalBERT (Li et al., 2020) for guided generation of Cause and Effect and the model introduced by Guan et al. (2020) for commonsense story generation.

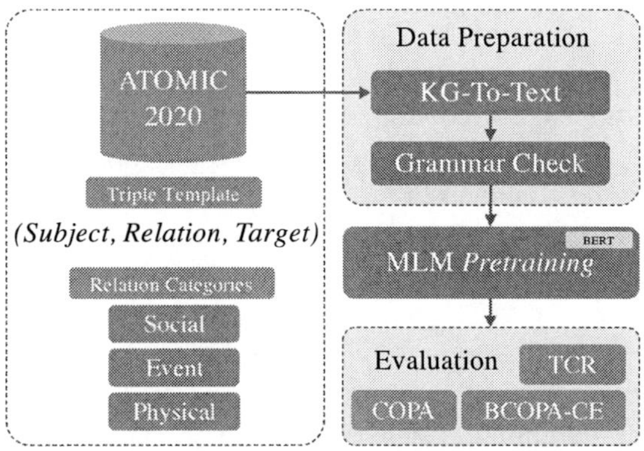

Figure 1: Overview of our proposed framework to continually pretrain PLMs with commonsense reasoning knowledge.

Motivated by the success of continual pretraining of PLMs for downstream tasks (Gururangan et al., 2020), we explore the impact of common sense knowledge injection as a form of continual pretraining for causal reasoning and *cause-effect* relation classification. It is worth highlighting that even though there are studies to show the efficacy of knowledge injection with continual pretraining for commonsense reasoning (Guan et al., 2020), performance of these techniques is very dependent on the domain and downstream tasks (Gururangan et al., 2020). And, to the best of our knowledge, there are limited studies on the effect of commonsense knowledge injection with knowledge graph data on cause-effect relation classification (Dalal

Proceedings of the First Workshop on Commonsense Representation and Reasoning (CSRR 2021), pages 43 - 48

et al., 2021). Our contributions are as follows:

- We study performance of PLMs augmented with knowledge graph data in the less investigated cause-effect relation classification task.
- We demonstrate that a simple masked language modeling framework using automatically verbalized knowledge graph triples, without any further model improvement (e.g., new architecture or loss function) or quality enhanced data for fine-tuning, can significantly boost the performance in cause-effect pair classification.
- We publicly release our knowledge graph verbalization codes and continually pretrained models.

2 Method

The overview of our method is shown in Figure 1.[1] We first convert triples in ATOMIC$^{20}_{20}$ (Hwang et al., 2021) knowledge graph to natural language texts. Then we continually pretrain BERT using Masked Language Modeling (MLM) and evaluate performance of the resulting model on different benchmarks. Samples in ATOMIC$^{20}_{20}$ are stored as triples in the form of *(head/subject, relation, tail/target)* in three splits including train, development, and test. ATOMIC$^{20}_{20}$ has 23 relation types that are classified into three categorical types including commonsense relations of social interactions, physical-entity commonsense relations, and event-centric commonsense relations. In the rest of the paper, we refer to these three categories as social, physical, and event, respectively.

2.1 Filtering Triples

We remove all duplicates and ignore all triples in which the target value is *none*. Moreover, we ignore all triples that include a blank. Since in masked language modeling we need to know the gold value of masked tokens, a triple that already has a blank (masked token/word) in it may not help our pretraining. For instance, in the triple: `[PersonX affords another ___, xAttr, useful]` it is hard to know why or understand what it means for a person to be useful without knowing what they afforded. This preprocessing step yields in 782,848 triples with 121,681, 177,706, and 483,461 from event, physical, and social categories, respectively. Distribution of these relations is shown in Figure 2.

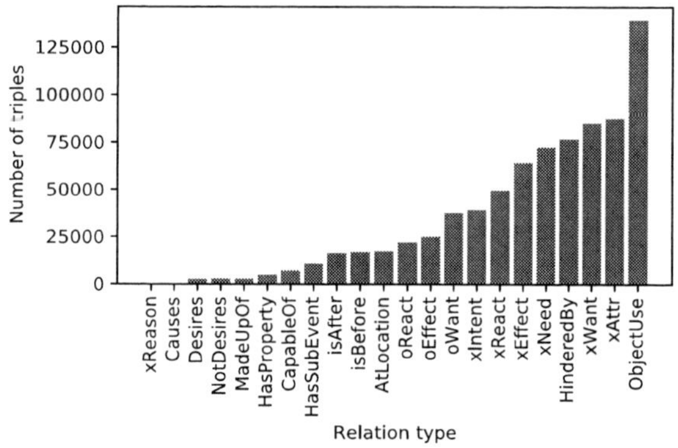

Figure 2: Distribution of relation types in ATOMIC$^{20}_{20}$.

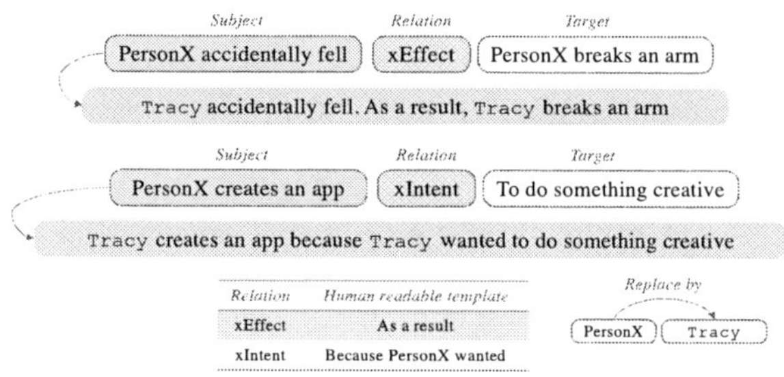

Figure 3: Examples of converting two triples in ATOMIC$^{20}_{20}$ to natural language text using human readable templates. Following Sap et al. (2019), we replace *PersonX* with a name.

2.2 Converting Triples

Each relation in ATOMIC$^{20}_{20}$ is associated with a human-readable template. For example, *xEffect*'s and *HasPrerequisite*'s templates are *as a result, PersonX will* and *to do this, one requires*, respectively. We use these templates to convert triples in ATOMIC$^{20}_{20}$ to sentences in natural language by concatenating the subject, relation template, and target. Examples of converting triples to text are shown in Figure 3.

2.3 Checking Grammar

When we convert triples to natural language text, ideally we want to have grammatically correct sentences. Human readable templates provided by ATOMIC$^{20}_{20}$ are not necessarily rendered in a way to form error-free sentences when concatenated with subject and target in a triple. To address this issue, we use an open-source grammar and spell

[1] Codes and models are publicly available at `https://github.com/phosseini/causal-reasoning`.

checker, LanguageTool,[2] to double-check our converted triples to ensure they do not contain obvious grammatical mistakes or spelling errors. Similar approaches that include deterministic grammatical transformations were also previously used to convert KG triples to coherent sentences (Davison et al., 2019). It is worth pointing out that the Data-To-Text generation (KG verbalization) for itself is a separate task and there have been efforts to address this task (Agarwal et al., 2021). We leave investigating the effects of using other Data-To-Text and grammar-checking methods to future research.

2.4 Continual Pretraining

As mentioned earlier, we use MLM to continually pretrain our PLM, *BERT-large-cased* (Devlin et al., 2018). We follow the same procedure as BERT to create the input data to our pretraining (e.g., number of tokens to mask in input examples). We run the pretraining using ATOMIC_{20}^{20}'s *train* and *development* splits as our training and evaluation sets, respectively, for 10 epochs on Google Colab TPU v2 using *PyTorch/XLA* package with a maximum sequence length of 30 and batch size of 128.[3] To avoid overfitting, we use early stopping with the patience of 3 on evaluation loss. We select the best model based on the lowest evaluation loss at the end of training.[4]

3 Experiments

3.1 Benchmarks

We chose multiple benchmarks of commonsense causal reasoning and cause-effect relation classification to ensure we thoroughly test the effects of our newly trained models. These benchmarks include: 1) Temporal and Causal Reasoning (TCR) dataset (Ning et al., 2018), a benchmark for joint reasoning of temporal and causal relations; 2) Choice Of Plausible Alternatives (COPA) (Roemmele et al., 2011) dataset which is a widely used and notable benchmark (Rogers et al., 2021) for commonsense causal reasoning; And 3) BCOPA-CE (Han and Wang, 2021), a new benchmark inspired by COPA, that contains unbiased token distributions which makes it a more challenging benchmark. For COPA-related experiments, since COPA does not have a training set, we use COPA's development set for fine-tuning our models and testing them on COPA's test set (COPA-test) and BCOPA-CE. For hyperparameter tuning, we randomly split COPA's development set into train (%90) and dev (%10) and find the best learning rate, batch size, and number of train epochs based on the evaluation accuracy on the development set. Then using COPA's original development set and best set of hyperparameters, we fine-tune our models and evaluate them on the test set. In all experiments, we report the average performance of models using four different random seeds. For TCR, we fine-tune and evaluate our models on train and test splits, respectively.

3.2 Models and Baseline

We use *bert-large-cased* pre-trained model in all experiments as our baseline. For COPA and BCOPA-CE, we convert all instances to a SWAG-formatted data (Zellers et al., 2018) and use Huggingface's *BertForMultipleChoice* –a BERT model with a multiple-choice classification head on top. And for TCR, we convert every instance by adding special tokens to input sequences as event boundaries and use the R-BERT [5] model (Wu and He, 2019). We chose R-BERT for our relation classification since it not only leverages the pretrained embeddings but also transfers information of target entities (e.g., events in a relation) through model's architecture and incorporates encodings of the targets entities. Examples of COPA and TCR are shown in Figure 4. BCOPA-CE has the same format as COPA.

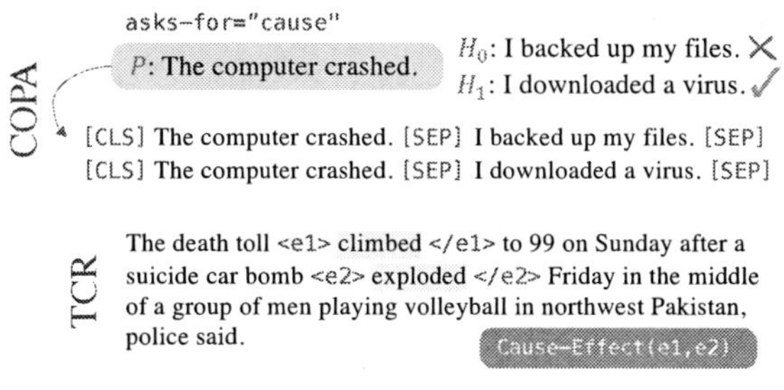

Figure 4: COPA and TCR examples. The COPA instance is converted to Multiple Choice format.

4 Results and Discussion

Results of our experiments on TCR are shown in Table 1. As can be seen, our model significantly outperforms both our baseline and the joint infer-

[2] https://tinyurl.com/yc77k3fb

[3] %99.99 of ATOMIC_{20}^{20} instances have 30 tokens or less.

[4] We use Huggingface's *BertForMaskedLM* implementation.

[5] We use the following implementation of R-BERT: https://github.com/monologg/R-BERT

ence framework by Ning et al. (2018) formulated as an integer linear programming (ILP) problem.

Model	Acc (%)
Joint system (Ning et al., 2018)	77.3
BERT-large (baseline) ✻	75.0
ATOMIC-BERT-large$_{MLM}$ ✻	**91.0**

Table 1: TCR Accuracy results. ✻ Our models

Results of experiments on COPA-test are shown in Table 2. We initially observed that a continually pretrained model using all three types of relations has a lower performance than our baseline. By taking a closer look at each relation type, we decided to train another model, this time only using the *event* relations. The reason is that event-centric relations in ATOMIC$^{20}_{20}$ specifically contain commonsense knowledge about event interaction for understating likely causal relations between events in the world (Hwang et al., 2021). In addition, event relations have a relatively longer context (# of tokens) than the average of all three relation types combined which means more context for a model to learn from. Our new pretrained model outperformed the baseline by nearly %5 which shows the effect of augmented pretrained language model with commonsense reasoning knowledge.

Model	Acc (%)
PMI (Roemmele et al., 2011)	58.8
b-l-*reg* (Han and Wang, 2021)	71.1
Google T5-base (Raffel et al., 2019)	71.2
BERT-large (Kavumba et al., 2019)	76.5
CausalBERT (Li et al., 2020)	78.6
BERT-SocialIQA (Sap et al., 2019)*	80.1
BERT-large (baseline) ✻	74.4
ATOMIC-BERT-large$_{MLM}$ ✻	
- Event only	79.2
Google T5-11B (Raffel et al., 2019)	94.8
DeBERTa-1.5B (He et al., 2020)	96.8

Table 2: COPA-test Accuracy results. ✻ Our models. * For a fair comparison, we report BERT-SocialIQA's average performance.

We further experiment on the *Easy* and *Hard* question splits in COPA-test separated by Kavumba et al. (2019) to see how our best model performs on harder questions that do not contain superficial cues. Results are shown in Table 3. As can be seen, our ATOMIC-BERT model significantly outperforms both the baseline and former models on Hard and Easy questions.

Model	Easy ↑	Hard ↑
(Han and Wang, 2021)	-	69.7
(Kavumba et al., 2019)	83.9	71.9
BERT-large (baseline) ✻	83.0	69.2
ATOMIC-BERT-large ✻	**88.9**	**73.1**

Table 3: COPA-test Accuracy results on Easy and Hard question subsets. ✻ Our models.

It is worth mentioning three points here. First, our model, BERT-large, has a significantly lower number of parameters than state-of-the-art models, Google T5-11B (~32x) and DeBERTa-1.5B (~4x) and it shows how smaller models can be competitive and benefit from continual pretraining. Second, we have not yet applied any model improvement methods such as using a margin-based loss introduced by Li et al. (2019) and used in Causal-BERT (Li et al., 2020), an extra regularization loss proposed by Han and Wang (2021), or fine-tuning with quality-enhanced training data, BCOPA, introduced by Kavumba et al. (2019). As a result, there is still great room to improve current models that can be a proper next step. Third, we achieved a performance on par with BERT-SocialIQA (Sap et al., 2019) [6] while we did not use crowdsourcing or any *manual* re-writing/correction, which is expensive, for verbalizing KG triples to create our pretraining data.

Model	Acc (%)
b-l-*aug* (Han and Wang, 2021)	51.1
b-l-*reg* (Han and Wang, 2021)	64.1
BERT-large (baseline) ✻	55.8
ATOMIC-BERT-large$_{MLM}$ ✻	
- Event only	58.1

Table 4: BCOPA-CE Accuracy results. ✻ Our models. * Base model in *b-l-** is BERT-large.

4.1 BCOPA-CE: Prompt vs. No Prompt

Results of experiments on BCOPA-CE are shown in Table 4. As expected based on the results also reported by Han and Wang (2021), we initially observed that our models are performing nearly as random baseline. Since we do not use the type of question when encoding input sequences, we decided to see whether adding question type as a prompt to input sequences will improve the performance. We added `It is because` and `As a`

[6] Our best random seed run achieved %81.4 accuracy.

`result`, as prompt for `asks-for="cause"` and `asks-for="effect"`, respectively. Interestingly, the new model outperforms the baseline and Han and Wang (2021)'s *b-l-aug* model that is fine-tuned with the same data as ours, when question types are added as prompts to input sequences of correct and incorrect answers in the test set. We also ran a similar experiment on COPA-test (Table 5) in which adding prompt did not help with performance improvement.

Train / Test	✗ Prompt	✓ Prompt
✗ Prompt	**79.2**	76.4
✓ Prompt	75.5	77.9

Table 5: COPA-test Accuracy ablation study results for prompt vs. no prompt.

5 Conclusion

We introduced a simple framework for augmenting PLMs with commonsense knowledge created by automatically verbalizing ATOMIC$^{20}_{20}$. Our results show that commonsense knowledge-augmented PLMs outperform the original PLMs on cause-effect pair classification and answering commonsense causal reasoning questions. As the next step, it would be interesting to see how the previously proposed model improvement methods or using unbiased fine-tuning datasets can potentially enhance the performance of our knowledge-augmented models.

References

Oshin Agarwal, Heming Ge, Siamak Shakeri, and Rami Al-Rfou. 2021. Knowledge graph based synthetic corpus generation for knowledge-enhanced language model pre-training. In *Proceedings of the 2021 Conference of the North American Chapter of the Association for Computational Linguistics: Human Language Technologies*, pages 3554–3565.

Eduardo Blanco, Nuria Castell, and Dan I Moldovan. 2008. Causal relation extraction. In *Lrec*.

Du-Seong Chang and Key-Sun Choi. 2004. Causal relation extraction using cue phrase and lexical pair probabilities. In *International Conference on Natural Language Processing*, pages 61–70. Springer.

Du-Seong Chang and Key-Sun Choi. 2006. Incremental cue phrase learning and bootstrapping method for causality extraction using cue phrase and word pair probabilities. *Information processing & management*, 42(3):662–678.

Dhairya Dalal, Mihael Arcan, and Paul Buitelaar. 2021. Enhancing multiple-choice question answering with causal knowledge. In *Proceedings of Deep Learning Inside Out (DeeLIO): The 2nd Workshop on Knowledge Extraction and Integration for Deep Learning Architectures*, pages 70–80.

Tirthankar Dasgupta, Rupsa Saha, Lipika Dey, and Abir Naskar. 2018. Automatic extraction of causal relations from text using linguistically informed deep neural networks. In *Proceedings of the 19th Annual SIGdial Meeting on Discourse and Dialogue*, pages 306–316.

Joe Davison, Joshua Feldman, and Alexander M Rush. 2019. Commonsense knowledge mining from pretrained models. In *Proceedings of the 2019 Conference on Empirical Methods in Natural Language Processing and the 9th International Joint Conference on Natural Language Processing (EMNLP-IJCNLP)*, pages 1173–1178.

Jacob Devlin, Ming-Wei Chang, Kenton Lee, and Kristina Toutanova. 2018. Bert: Pre-training of deep bidirectional transformers for language understanding. *arXiv preprint arXiv:1810.04805*.

Quang Xuan Do, Yee Seng Chan, and Dan Roth. 2011. Minimally supervised event causality identification. In *Proceedings of the Conference on Empirical Methods in Natural Language Processing*, pages 294–303. Association for Computational Linguistics.

Jesse Dunietz, Jaime G Carbonell, and Lori Levin. 2018. Deepcx: A transition-based approach for shallow semantic parsing with complex constructional triggers. In *Proceedings of the 2018 Conference on Empirical Methods in Natural Language Processing*, pages 1691–1701.

Lei Gao, Prafulla Kumar Choubey, and Ruihong Huang. 2019. Modeling document-level causal structures for event causal relation identification. In *Proceedings of the 2019 Conference of the North American Chapter of the Association for Computational Linguistics: Human Language Technologies, Volume 1 (Long and Short Papers)*, pages 1808–1817.

Daniela Garcia et al. 1997. Coatis, an nlp system to locate expressions of actions connected by causality links. In *International Conference on Knowledge Engineering and Knowledge Management*, pages 347–352. Springer.

Roxana Girju. 2003. Automatic detection of causal relations for question answering. In *Proceedings of the ACL 2003 workshop on Multilingual summarization and question answering-Volume 12*, pages 76–83. Association for Computational Linguistics.

Jian Guan, Fei Huang, Zhihao Zhao, Xiaoyan Zhu, and Minlie Huang. 2020. A knowledge-enhanced pretraining model for commonsense story generation. *Transactions of the Association for Computational Linguistics*, 8:93–108.

Suchin Gururangan, Ana Marasović, Swabha Swayamdipta, Kyle Lo, Iz Beltagy, Doug Downey, and Noah A Smith. 2020. Don't stop pretraining: Adapt language models to domains and tasks. In *Proceedings of the 58th Annual Meeting of the Association for Computational Linguistics*, pages 8342–8360.

Mingyue Han and Yinglin Wang. 2021. Doing good or doing right? exploring the weakness of commonsense causal reasoning models. In *Proceedings of the 59th Annual Meeting of the Association for Computational Linguistics and the 11th International Joint Conference on Natural Language Processing (Volume 2: Short Papers)*, pages 151–157, Online. Association for Computational Linguistics.

Chikara Hashimoto, Kentaro Torisawa, Stijn De Saeger, Jong-Hoon Oh, and Jun'ichi Kazama. 2012. Excitatory or inhibitory: A new semantic orientation extracts contradiction and causality from the web. In *Proceedings of the 2012 Joint Conference on Empirical Methods in Natural Language Processing and Computational Natural Language Learning*, pages 619–630. Association for Computational Linguistics.

Pengcheng He, Xiaodong Liu, Jianfeng Gao, and Weizhu Chen. 2020. Deberta: Decoding-enhanced bert with disentangled attention. *arXiv preprint arXiv:2006.03654*.

Christopher Hidey and Kathy McKeown. 2016. Identifying causal relations using parallel Wikipedia articles. In *Proceedings of the 54th Annual Meeting of the Association for Computational Linguistics (Volume 1: Long Papers)*, pages 1424–1433, Berlin, Germany. Association for Computational Linguistics.

Jena D. Hwang, Chandra Bhagavatula, Ronan Le Bras, Jeff Da, Keisuke Sakaguchi, Antoine Bosselut, and Yejin Choi. 2021. Comet-atomic 2020: On symbolic and neural commonsense knowledge graphs. In *AAAI*.

Leo Joskowicz, T Ksiezyck, and Ralph Grishman. 1989. Deep domain models for discourse analysis. In *[1989] Proceedings. The Annual AI Systems in Government Conference*, pages 195–200. IEEE.

Randy M Kaplan and Genevieve Berry-Rogghe. 1991. Knowledge-based acquisition of causal relationships in text. *Knowledge Acquisition*, 3(3):317–337.

Pride Kavumba, Naoya Inoue, Benjamin Heinzerling, Keshav Singh, Paul Reisert, and Kentaro Inui. 2019. When choosing plausible alternatives, clever hans can be clever. *EMNLP 2019*, page 33.

Christopher SG Khoo, Jaklin Kornfilt, Robert N Oddy, and Sung Hyon Myaeng. 1998. Automatic extraction of cause-effect information from newspaper text without knowledge-based inferencing. *Literary and Linguistic Computing*, 13(4):177–186.

Zhongyang Li, Tongfei Chen, and Benjamin Van Durme. 2019. Learning to rank for plausible plausibility. In *Proceedings of the 57th Annual Meeting of the Association for Computational Linguistics*, pages 4818–4823.

Zhongyang Li, Xiao Ding, Ting Liu, J Edward Hu, and Benjamin Van Durme. 2020. Guided generation of cause and effect. IJCAI.

Qiang Ning, Zhili Feng, Hao Wu, and Dan Roth. 2018. Joint reasoning for temporal and causal relations. In *Proceedings of the 56th Annual Meeting of the Association for Computational Linguistics (Volume 1: Long Papers)*, pages 2278–2288, Melbourne, Australia. Association for Computational Linguistics.

Jeffrey Pennington, Richard Socher, and Christopher D Manning. 2014. Glove: Global vectors for word representation. In *Proceedings of the 2014 conference on empirical methods in natural language processing (EMNLP)*, pages 1532–1543.

Colin Raffel, Noam Shazeer, Adam Roberts, Katherine Lee, Sharan Narang, Michael Matena, Yanqi Zhou, Wei Li, and Peter J Liu. 2019. Exploring the limits of transfer learning with a unified text-to-text transformer. *arXiv preprint arXiv:1910.10683*.

Melissa Roemmele, Cosmin Adrian Bejan, and Andrew S Gordon. 2011. Choice of plausible alternatives: An evaluation of commonsense causal reasoning. In *2011 AAAI Spring Symposium Series*.

Anna Rogers, Matt Gardner, and Isabelle Augenstein. 2021. Qa dataset explosion: A taxonomy of nlp resources for question answering and reading comprehension. *arXiv preprint arXiv:2107.12708*.

Maarten Sap, Hannah Rashkin, Derek Chen, Ronan Le Bras, and Yejin Choi. 2019. Social IQa: Commonsense reasoning about social interactions. In *Proceedings of the 2019 Conference on Empirical Methods in Natural Language Processing and the 9th International Joint Conference on Natural Language Processing (EMNLP-IJCNLP)*, pages 4463–4473, Hong Kong, China. Association for Computational Linguistics.

Shanchan Wu and Yifan He. 2019. Enriching pre-trained language model with entity information for relation classification. In *Proceedings of the 28th ACM international conference on information and knowledge management*, pages 2361–2364.

Rowan Zellers, Yonatan Bisk, Roy Schwartz, and Yejin Choi. 2018. Swag: A large-scale adversarial dataset for grounded commonsense inference. In *Proceedings of the 2018 Conference on Empirical Methods in Natural Language Processing*, pages 93–104.

CURIE: An Iterative Querying Approach for Reasoning About Situations

Dheeraj Rajagopal *, Aman Madaan *, Niket Tandon†, Yiming Yang,
Shrimai Prabhumoye, Abhilasha Ravichander, Peter Clark†, Eduard Hovy
Language Technologies Institute, Carnegie Mellon University
† Allen Institute for Artificial Intelligence
{dheeraj,amadaan,yiming,sprabhum,aravicha,hovy}@cs.cmu.edu
{nikett, peterc}@allenai.org

Abstract

Predicting the effects of unexpected situations is an important reasoning task, e.g., would cloudy skies help or hinder plant growth? Given a context, the goal of such situational reasoning is to elicit the consequences of a new situation (*st*) that arises in that context. We propose CURIE, a method to iteratively build a graph of relevant consequences explicitly in a structured situational graph (*st* graph) using natural language queries over a fine-tuned language model. Across multiple domains, CURIE generates *st* graphs that humans find relevant and meaningful in eliciting the consequences of a new situation (75% of the graphs were judged correct by humans). We present a case study of a situation reasoning end task (WIQA-QA), where simply augmenting their input with *st* graphs improves accuracy by 3 points. We show that these improvements mainly come from a hard subset of the data, that requires background knowledge and multi-hop reasoning.

1 Introduction

A long-standing challenge in reasoning is to model the consequences of an unseen situation in a context. In the real world unexpected situations are common. Machines capable of situational reasoning are crucial because they are expected to gracefully handle such unexpected situations. For example, when eating leftover food, would it be more safer from virus if we microwave the food? - answering this requires understanding the complex events *virus contamination* and *effect of heat on virus*. Much of this information remains implicit (by Grice's maxim of quantity (Grice, 1975)), thus requiring inference.

Recently, NLP literature has shown renewed interest in situational reasoning with applications in qualitative reasoning (Tandon et al., 2019; Tafjord et al., 2019), physical commonsense reasoning (Sap et al., 2019; Bisk et al., 2020), and defeasible inference (Rudinger et al., 2020). These tasks take as input a context providing background information, a situation (*st*), and an ending, and predict the reachability from *st* to that ending. However, these systems have three limitations: (i) systems trained on these tasks are often domain specific, (ii) these tasks do not require a supporting structure that elicits the dynamics of the reasoning process, and (iii) these tasks are addressed as a classification problem restricting to a closed vocabulary setting.

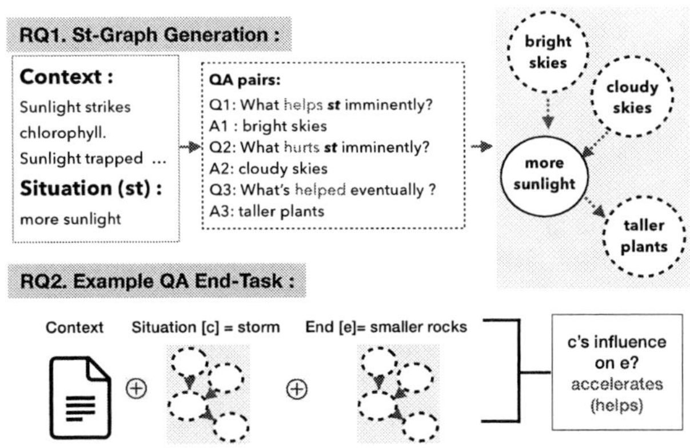

Figure 1: **RQ1**: CURIE generates situational graphs by iteratively querying a model, making explicit the model's knowledge of effects of influences (+ve / -ve). **RQ2**: Situational graphs improve situational reasoning QA when appended to the question context.

To address these limitations, we propose CURIE- a system to iteratively query pretrained language models to *generate* an explicit structured graph of consequences, that we call a *situational reasoning graph* (*st*-graph). The task is illustrated in Figure 1: given some context and situation *st* (short phrase), our system generates a *st*-graph based on the contextual knowledge. CURIE supports the following kinds of reasoning:

- If a situation *st* occurs, which event is

* authors contributed equally to this work. Ordering determined by dice rolling.

Proceedings of the First Workshop on Commonsense Representation and Reasoning (CSRR 2021), pages 49 - 63

more/less likely to happen imminently/ eventually?

- Which event will support/ prevent situation *st* from happening imminently/ eventually?

As shown in Figure 1, our approach to this task is to iteratively compile the answers to questions 1 and 2 to construct the *st*-graph where imminent/eventual capture multihop reasoning questions. Compared to a free-form text output obtained from an out-of-the-box sequence-to-sequence model, our approach gives more control and flexibility over the graph generation process, including arbitrarily reasoning for any particular node in the graph. The generated *st*-graphs are of high quality as judged by humans for correctness. In addition to human evaluation, we also show that a downstream task that requires reasoning about situations can compose natural language queries to construct a *st*-reasoning graph via CURIE. The resulting *st*-graph can be simply augmented to their input to achieve performance gains, specifically on the subset of hard questions that require background knowledge and multihop reasoning. In summary, this paper addresses the following research questions:

RQ1: Given a context and a situation, how can we generate a situational reasoning (*st*) graph? To answer RQ1, we present CURIE, the first domain-agnostic situational reasoning system that takes as input a context and a situation *st* and iteratively generates a situational reasoning graph (§2). Our system is effective at situational reasoning across three datasets as validated by human evaluation and automated metrics.

RQ2: Can the *st*-graphs generated by CURIE improve performance of a downstream task? To answer RQ2, we show that *st* graphs generated by CURIE improve a *st*-reasoning task (WIQA-QA) by 3 points on accuracy by simply augmenting their input with our generated situational graphs, especially for a hard subset that requires background knowledge and multi-hop reasoning (§4).

2 CURIE for Situational Reasoning

CURIE provides both a general framework for situational reasoning and a method for constructing *st*-reasoning graphs from pretrained language models.

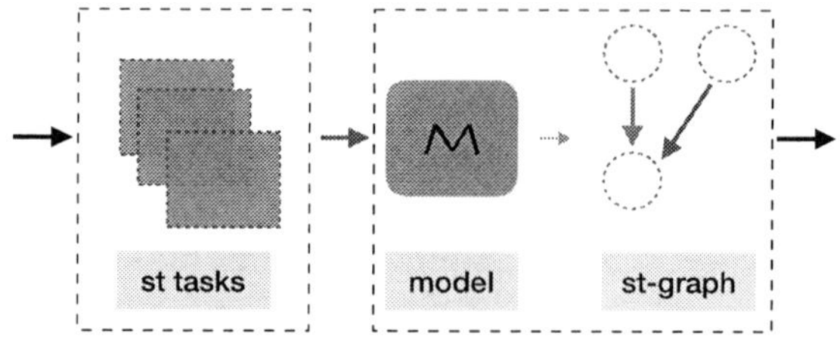

Figure 2: CURIE framework consists of two components: (i) a formulation that adapts datasets that allow *st*-reasoning for pretraining (ii) a method to iteratively build structured *st*-graphs using natural language queries over a fine-tuned language model ($\mathcal{M}$).

Figure 2 shows the overall architecture of CURIE. CURIE framework consists of two components: (i) *st-reasoning task formulation :* a formulation that adapts datasets that allow situational reasoning (ii) *st-graph construction :* a method to fine-tune language model $\mathcal{M}$ to generate the consequences of a situation and iteratively construct structured situational graphs (shown in Figure 1). In this section, we present (i) our task formulation (§2.1), (ii) adapting existing datasets for CURIE task formulation (§2.2), (iii) the learning procedure (§2.3), and (iv) the *st*-graph generation process (§2.4).

2.1 Task Formulation

We describe the general task formulation for adapting pretraining language models to the *st*-reasoning task. Given a context $T = \{s_1, s_2, \ldots, s_N\}$ comprising of N sentences, and a situation *st*, our goal is to generate an *st*-graph G that captures the effects of situation *st*.

An *st*-graph $G(V, E)$ is an unweighted directed acyclic graph. A vertex $v \in V$ is an event or a state that describes a change to the original conditions in T. Each edge $e_{ij} \in E$ is labeled with a relationship r_{ij}, that indicates whether v_i *positively* or *negatively* influences v_j. Positive influences are represented via green edges comprising one of {*entails, strengthens, helps*} and negative influences represented via red edges that depict one of {*contradicts, weakens, hurts*}. Our relation set is general and can accommodate various *st*-reasoning tasks. Given two nodes $v_i, v_k \in V$, if a path from v_i to v_k has more than one edge, we describe the effect c as *eventual* and a direct effect as *imminent.*

We derive the training data by transforming a repository of (context T, *st*-graph G) tuples into a set of question-answer pairs. Each pair of vertices $v_s, v_t \in G$ that are connected by a path contribute

Dataset	Original formulation	Original *st* graph	Iterative formulation (*st*)
WIQA	*context*: Wind creates waves.. Waves wash on beaches... *ques*: If there is storm, how will it affect bigger waves? *explanation*: storm → stronger wind → bigger waves *answer*: helps bigger waves	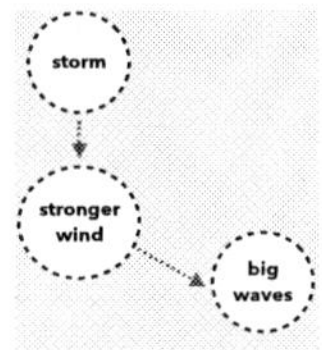	Given *context* and *st*: there is a storm Q1: What does *st* help *imminently* ? A1: stronger wind Q2: What does *st* help *eventually* ? A2: bigger waves
QUAREL	*context*: Car rolls further on wood than on thick carpet *ques*: what has more resistance? (a) wood (b) the carpet *simplified logical form of context, ques*: distance is higher on wood → (a) friction is higher in carpet (or) (b) friction is higher in wood *answer*: (b) the carpet	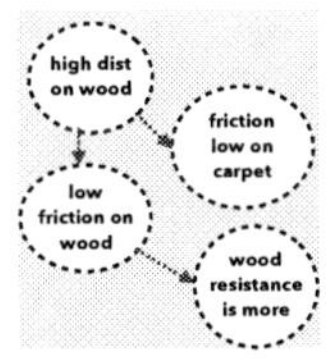	Given *context* and *st*: distance is higher on wood Q1: What does *st* entail *imminently* ? A1: friction is lower in wood Q2: What does *st* contradict *imminently* ? A2: friction is lower in carpet Q3: What does *st* entail *eventually* ? A3: wood has more resistance
DEFEAS	*context*: Two men and a dog are standing among the green hills. *hypothesis*: The men are farmers. *update1*: The dog is a sheep dog strengthens hypothesis *update2*: Men with tour map weakens hypothesis	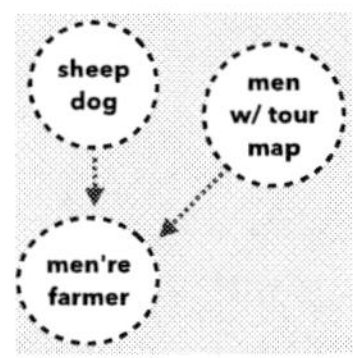	Given *context* and *st*: dog is a sheep dog Q1: What does *st* strengthen *imminently* ? A1: The men are farmers *st*: men are studying tour maps Q2: What does *st* weaken *imminently*? A2: The men are farmers

Table 1: The datasets used by CURIE and how we re-purpose them for *st* reasoning graph generation task. As explained in §2.1, the green edges set depicts relation (r) (entail, strengthen, helps) and red edges depict one of (contradict, weaken, hurts). The { *imminent*, *eventual* } effects (c) are used to support multihop reasoning. DEFEAS = DEFEASIBLE, *chain* refers to reasoning chain. Some examples are cut to fit. The key insight is that an *st*-graph can be decomposed into a series of QA pairs, enabling us to leverage seq-to-seq approaches for *st*-reasoning.

one question-answer pair to the training data for CURIE, such that every question comprises of: i) context T, ii) a *st*-vertex v_s, iii) a relation r, and iv) the nature of the effect c and the answer is the target node v_t. An example is shown in Figure 1. Compared to an end-to-end approach to graph generation, our approach gives more flexibility over the generation process, enabling reasoning for any chosen node in the graph. Thus the training data consists of tuples $(\mathbf{x}_i, \mathbf{y}_i)$, with $\mathbf{x}_i = (T, v_s, r, c)_i$ and $\mathbf{y}_i$ is the target situation v_t.

2.2 Generalizing Existing Datasets

Despite theoretical advances, lack of a large-scale general situational reasoning dataset presents a challenge to train seq-to-seq language models. We describe how we generalize existing diverse datasets towards *st*-reasoning towards finetuning a language model $\mathcal{M}$. If a reasoning dataset contains a context, a *st*-situation and can describe the influence of *st* in terms of green and/or red edges, it can be seamlessly adapted to CURIE framework. Due to the lack of existing datasets that directly support our task formulation, we adapt the following three diverse datasets - WIQA, QUAREL and DEFEASIBLE for CURIE (dataset statistics in Table 3).

WIQA: WIQA task studies the effect of a perturbation in a procedural text (Tandon et al., 2019). The context T is a procedural text describing a physical process, and *st* is a perturbation i.e., an external situation deviating from T, and the effect of *st* is either helps or hurts. See Table 1 for examples.

QUAREL: QUAREL dataset (Tafjord et al., 2019) contains qualitative story questions where T is a narrative, and *st* is a qualitative statement. T and *st* are also expressed in a simpler, logical form, which we use as it highlights the reasoning challenge. The effect of *st* is entails or contradicts (see Table 1).

Research question	Training dataset	Test dataset	Task	Metrics
Can we generate good *st* graphs? (§3)	WIQA-*st*	WIQA-*st*	generation	ROUGE, BLEU
	QUAREL-*st*	QUAREL-*st*	generation	ROUGE, BLEU
	DEFEASIBLE-*st*	DEFEASIBLE-*st*	generation	ROUGE, BLEU
Can we improve downstream tasks? (§4.1)	WIQA-*st*, WIQA-QA	WIQA-QA	finetuned QA	accuracy

Table 2: Overview of experiments

Dataset	train	dev	test
WIQA	119.2k	34.8k	34.8k
QUAREL	4.6k	1.3k	652
DEFEASIBLE	200k	14.9k	15.4k

Table 3: Dataset wise statistics, we maintain the splits

DEFEASIBLE: The DEFEASIBLE reasoning task (Rudinger et al., 2020) studies inference in the presence of a counterfactual. The context T is a premise describing an everyday context, and the situation *st* is an observed evidence which either strengthens or weakens the hypothesis. We adapt the original abductive setup as shown in Table 1. In addition to commonsense situations, DEFEASIBLE-*st* also comprises of social situations, thereby contributing to the diversity of our datasets.

Algorithm 1: ITERATIVEGRAPHGEN (IGEN): generating *st* graphs with CURIE

Given: CURIE language model $\mathcal{M}$.
Given: Context T, situation *st*, a set $R = \{(r_i, c_i)\}_{i=1}^{N_Q}$ of N_Q (r, c) tuples.
Result: *st* graph G: i^{th} node is generated with relation r_i, effect type c_i.
Init: $G \leftarrow \emptyset$
for $i \leftarrow 1, 2, \ldots, N_Q$ **do**
  /* Create a query */
  $\mathbf{x}_i = \texttt{concat}(T, st, r_i, c_i)$;
  /* Sample a node from $\mathcal{M}$ */
  $\mathbf{y}_i \sim \mathcal{M}(\mathbf{x}_i)$;
  /* Add sampled node, edge */
  $G = G \cup (r_i, c_i, \mathbf{y}_i)$;
end
return G

2.3 Learning to Generate *st*-graphs

To reiterate our task formulation (§2.1), for a given context and *st*, we first specify a set of questions and the resulting outputs for the questions is then compiled to form a *st*-graph.

The training data consists of tuples $(\mathbf{x}_i, \mathbf{y}_i)$, with $\mathbf{x}_i = (T, st, r, c)_i$ where T denotes the context, *st* the situation, r is the edge (green or red), c indicates the nature of the effect (imminent or eventual), and $\mathbf{y}_i$ is the output (a short sentence or a phrase depicting the effect). The output of N_Q such questions is compiled into a graph $G = \{\mathbf{y}_i\}_{1:N_Q}$ (Fig. 1).

We use a pretrained language model $\mathcal{M}$ to estimate the probability of generating an answer $\mathbf{y}_i$ for an input $\mathbf{x}_i$. We first transform the tuple $\mathbf{x}_i = \langle x_i^1, x_i^2, \ldots, x_i^N \rangle$ into a single query sequence of tokens by concatenating its components i.e. $\mathbf{x}_i = \texttt{concat}(T, st, r, c)$, where concat is string concatenation. Let the sequence of tokens representing the target event be $\mathbf{y}_i = \langle y_i^1, y_i^2, \ldots, y_i^M \rangle$, where N and M are the lengths of the query and the target event sequences. We model the conditional probability $p_\theta(\mathbf{y}_i \mid \mathbf{x}_i)$ as a series of conditional next token distributions parameterized by θ: as $p_\theta(\mathbf{y}_i \mid \mathbf{x}_i) = \prod_{k=1}^{M} p_\theta(y_i^k \mid \mathbf{x}_i, y_i^1, .., y_i^{k-1})$.

2.4 Inference to Decode *st*-graphs

The auto-regressive factorization of the language model p_θ allows us to efficiently generate target event influences for a given test input $\mathbf{x}_j$. The process of decoding begins by sampling the first token $y_j^1 \sim p_\theta(y \mid \mathbf{x}_j)$. The next token is then drawn by sampling $y_j^2 \sim p_\theta(y \mid \mathbf{x}_j, y_j^1)$. The process is repeated until a specified *end-symbol* token is drawn at the Kth step. We use nucleus sampling (Holtzman et al., 2019) in practice. The tokens $\langle y_j^1, y_j^2, \ldots, y_j^{K-1} \rangle$ are then returned as the generated answer. To generate the final *st*-reasoning graph G, we combine all the generated answers $\{\mathbf{y}_i\}_{1:N_Q}$ that had the same context and *st* pair (T, st) over all (r, c) combinations. We can then use generated answer $st' \in \{\mathbf{y}_i\}_{1:N_Q}$, as a new input to $\mathcal{M}$ as (T, st') to recursively expand the *st*-graph to arbitrary depth and structures (Algorithm 1). One such instance of using CURIE *st* graphs for a downstream QA task is shown in §4.

3 RQ1: Establishing Baselines for *st*-graph Generation

This section reports on the quality of the generated *st* reasoning graphs and establishes strong baseline scores for *st*-graph generation. We use the datasets described in section §2.2 for our experiments.

Model ($\mathcal{M}$)	BLEU	ROUGE
WIQA-*st*		
LSTM Seq-to-Seq	7.51	18.71
GPT ~(w/o T)	7.82	19.30
GPT-2 ~(w/o T)	10.01	20.93
GPT	9.95	19.64
GPT-2	**16.23**	**29.65**
QUAREL-*st*		
LSTM Seq-to-Seq	13.05	24.76
GPT ~(w/o T)	20.20	36.64
GPT-2 ~(w/o T)	26.98	41.14
GPT	25.48	42.87
GPT-2	**35.20**	**50.57**
DEFEASIBLE-*st*		
LSTM Seq-to-Seq	7.84	17.50
GPT ~(w/o T)	9.91	20.63
GPT-2 ~(w/o T)	9.17	9.43
GPT	10.49	**21.79**
GPT-2	**10.52**	21.19

Table 4: Generation results for CURIE with baselines for language model $\mathcal{M}$. We find that context is essential for performance (w/o T). We provide these baseline scores as a reference for future research.

3.1 Baseline Language Models

To reiterate, CURIE is composed of (i) task formulation component and (ii) graph construction component, that uses a language model $\mathcal{M}$ to construct the *st*-graph. We want to emphasize that any language model architecture can be a candidate for $\mathcal{M}$. Since our *st*-task formulation is novel, we establish strong baselines over the three datasets. Our experiments include large-scale language models (LSTM and pretrained transformer) with varying parameter sizes and pre-training, and the corresponding ablation studies. Our choices for $\mathcal{M}$ are:

LSTM Seq-to-Seq: We train an LSTM (Hochreiter and Schmidhuber, 1997) based sequence to sequence model (Bahdanau et al., 2015) which uses global attention described in (Luong et al., 2015). We initialize the embedding layer with pre-trained 300 dimensional Glove (Pennington et al., 2014)[1]. We use 2 layers of LSTM encoder and decoder with a hidden size of 500. The encoder is bidirectional.

GPT: We use the original design of GPT (Radford et al., 2018) with 12 layers, 768-dimensional hidden states, and 12 attention heads.

GPT-2: We use the medium (355M) variant of GPT-2 (Radford et al., 2019) with 24 layers, 1024 hidden size, 16 attention heads. For both GPT and GPT-2, we initialize the model with the pre-trained weights and use the implementation provided by Wolf et al. (2019).

We use Adam (Kingma and Ba, 2014) for optimization with a learning rate of $5e-05$. All the dropouts (Srivastava et al., 2014) were set to 0.1. We found the best hyperparameter settings by searching the space using the following hyperparameters.

1. embedding dropout = {0.1, 0.2, 0.3}
2. learning rate = {1e-05, 2e-05, 5e-05, 1e-06}

We compare the *st*-graphs generated by various language models with the gold-standard reference graphs. To compare the two graphs, we first flatten both the reference graph and the *st*-graph as text sequences and then compute the overlap between them. Due to a lack of strong automated metrics, we use the commonly used evaluation metrics for generation BLEU (Papineni et al., 2002), and ROUGE (Lin, 2004) [2]. Our results shown in Table 4 indicate that the task of *st* generation is challenging, and suggests that incorporating *st*-reasoning specific inductive biases might be beneficial. At the same time, Table 4 shows that even strong models like GPT-2 achieve low BLEU and ROUGE scores (specifically on WIQA and DEFEASIBLE), leaving a lot of room for model improvements in the future.

We also show ablation results for the model with respect to the context T (§2.1), by fine-tuning without the context. We find that context is essential for performance for both GPT and GPT-2 (indicated with w/o T in Table 4). Further, we note that the gains achieved by adding context are higher for GPT-2, hinting that larger models can more effectively utilize the context[3].

[1] https://github.com/OpenNMT/OpenNMT-py
[2] https://github.com/Maluuba/nlg-eval
[3] More qualitative examples shown in appendix B

Error category	%	Example question	Reference	Predicted
Polarity	7%	What does 'oil fields over-used' help eventually ?	there is not oil refined	more oil is refined
Linguistic Variability	27%	What does 'rabbits will not become pregnant' hurt imminently ?	more rabbits	more babies
Related Event	23%	What does 'inhaling more air from the outside' hurt imminently ?	there will be less oxygen in your blood	you develop more blood clo- -ts in your veins
Wrong	40%	What does 'nutrients are unavailable for plants' hurt eventually ?	more plants	more wine being produced
Erroneous Reference	3%	What does 'rabbit are not mating' hurt imminently?	less rabbits	more babies

Table 5: Canonical examples per error category. Error analysis is only shown for the incorrect outputs. For polarity errors, we use guidelines shown in appendix A.1

3.2 Human Evaluation

N-gram metrics such as BLEU and ROUGE are known to be limited, specifically for reasoning tasks. Further, we observe from Table 4 that context is crucial for generation quality. To better understand this effect, we perform human evaluation on a random sample from the dev set to compare GPT-2- w/o T and GPT-2 models. Our goal is to assess quality of generations, and the importance of grounding generations in context. Four human judges annotated 100 unique samples for *correctness*, *relevance* and *reference*, described next.

Correctness: We conducted a human evaluation to evaluate the correctness of the generated graphs where we aggregated nodes for a given *st*. The user interface for the annotation (shown in Figure 3) displayed the context T and the corresponding graph G generated by GPT-2 using Algorithm 1. The human judges were asked to annotate the nodes, edges, and the overall graph for correctness. A graph was labeled as correct if either a) all the nodes and edges were correct, or b) the graph had a minor issue that the judges deem not detrimental to the overall correctness. The inter-annotator agreement on graph correctness was substantial with a Fleiss' Kappa score (Fleiss and Cohen, 1973) of 0.69. Table 6 shows that human judges rated >75% of the graphs to be correct given the context, showing that CURIE generates high-quality graphs for a diverse set of contexts.

Relevance: The annotators are provided with the context T, the situation *st*, and the relational questions. The annotators were asked, "Which system (A or B) is more accurate relative to the background information given in the context?" They could also pick option C (no preference). The order of the references was randomized. Table 7 (row 1) shows that GPT-2 outperforms GPT-2 (w/o T), confirming our hypothesis that context is important as GPT-2 generates target events that are grounded in the passage and source events.

Attribute	Node	Edge	Graph
% Correct	79.71	77.78	75.36

Table 6: Human Analysis of Graph Correctness. About 75% of the graphs were deemed as *correct*.

Task	GPT-2 (w/o T)	GPT-2	No Preference
Relevance	23.05	46.11	30.83
Reference	11.67	31.94	56.39

Table 7: Results of human evaluation. The numbers show the percentage(%) of times a particular option was selected for each metric.

Reference: We measure how accurately each system-generated event reflects the reference (true) event. Here, the annotators saw only the reference sentence and the outputs of two systems (A and B) in a randomized order. We asked the annotators, "Which system's output is closest in meaning to the reference?" The annotators could pick the options A, B, or C (no preference). Table 7 (row 2) illus-

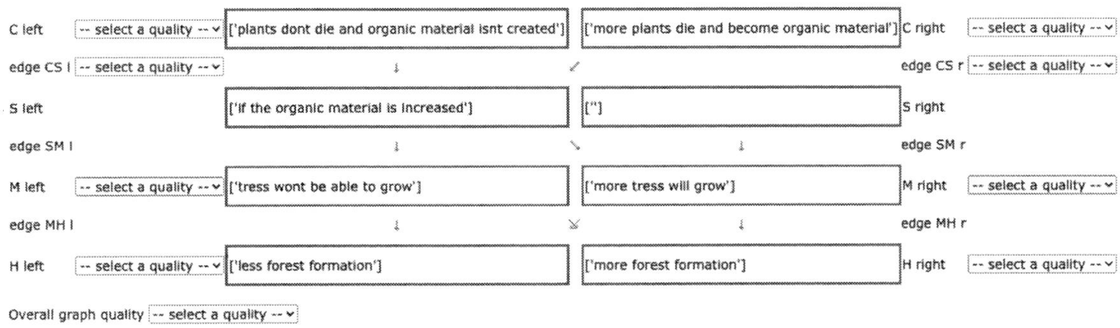

Figure 3: User interface for graph correctness evaluation. The human judges were asked to rate the if the the generated nodes, edges, and the overall graph are correct for the given context. The paragraph for this example was: *Grass and small plants grow in an area. These plants die. The soil gains organic material. The soil becomes more fertile. Larger plants are able to be supported. Trees eventually grow.*

trates that the output generated by `GPT-2` is closer in meaning to the reference compared to `GPT-2` (w/o T) reinforcing the importance of context.

Both the models (with and without context) produced similarly grammatically fluent outputs.

3.3 Error Analysis

The reference and relevance task scores together show that `GPT-2` does not generate target events that are exactly similar to the reference target events, but are correct in the context of the passage and source event. To investigate this, we analyze a random sample of 100 points from the dev set. Out of the erroneous samples, we observe the following error categories (shown in Table 5):

- **Polarity (7%)**: Predicted polarity was wrong but the event was correct.
- **Linguistic Variability (27%)**: Output was a linguistic variant of the reference.
- **Related event (23%)**: Output was related but different reference expected.
- **Wrong (40%)**: Output was fully unrelated.
- **Erroneous reference (3%)**: Gold annotations themselves were erroneous.

3.4 Consistency Analysis

Finally, we measure if the generated *st*-graphs are consistent. Consider a path of length two in the generated *st*-graph (say, A $\rightarrow$ B $\rightarrow$ C). A consistent graph would have identical answers to *what does A help eventually* i.e., "C", and *what does B help imminently* i.e., "C". To analyze consistency, we manually evaluated 50 random generated length-two paths, selected from WIQA-*st* dev set. We observe that 58% samples had consistent output w.r.t the generated output. We also measure consistency w.r.t. the gold standard (the true outputs in the dev set), and observe that the system output is $\approx$48% consistent. Despite being trained on independent samples, *st*-graphs show reasonable consistency and improving consistency further is an interesting future research direction.

3.5 Discussion

In summary, CURIE allows adapting pretrained language models to generate *st*-graphs that humans meaningful and relevant with a high degree of correctness. We also perform an in-depth analysis of the errors of CURIE. We establish multiple baselines with diverse language models to guide future research. We show that context is more important than model size for *st*-reasoning tasks.

4 RQ2: CURIE for Downstream Tasks

In this section, we describe the approach for augmenting *st* graphs for downstream reasoning tasks. We first identify the choice of tasks (*st*-tasks) for domain adaptive pretraining (Gururangan et al., 2020) and obtain CURIE language model $\mathcal{M}$ (based on `GPT-2`). The downstream task then provides input context, *st* and (relation, type) tuples of interest, and obtains the *st*-graphs (see Algorithm 1) from CURIE. We describe one such instantiation in §4.1.

4.1 CURIE augmented WIQA-QA

We examine the utility of CURIE-generated graphs in the WIQA-QA (Tandon et al., 2019) downstream question answering benchmark. Input to this task is a context supplied in form of a passage T, a starting event c, an ending event e, and the output is a label {*helps*, *hurts*, or *no_effect*} depicting how the ending e is influenced by the event c.

We hypothesize that CURIE can augment c and e with their influences, giving a more comprehensive scenario than the context alone. We use CURIE trained on WIQA-*st* to augment the event influences in each sample in the QA task as additional context. We obtain the influence graphs for c and e by defining R_{fwd} = {(*helps*, *imminent*), (*hurts*, *imminent*) } and R_{rev} = { (*helped by*, *imminent*), (*hurt by*, *imminent*)}, and using algorithm 1 as follows:

$$G(c) = \texttt{IGEN}(T, c, R_{fwd})$$
$$G(e) = \texttt{IGEN}(T, e, R_{rev})$$

We hypothesize that WIQA-*st* graphs are able to generate reasoning chains that connect c to e, even if e is not an immediate consequence of c. Following Tandon et al. (2019), we encode the input sequence $\texttt{concat}(T, c, e)$ using the BERT encoder E (Devlin et al., 2019), and use the [CLS] token representation ($\hat{\mathbf{h}}_i$) as our sequence representation.

We then use the same encoder E to encode the generated effects $\texttt{concat}(G(c), G(e))$, and use the [CLS] token to get a representation for augmented c and e ($\hat{\mathbf{h}}_a$). Following the encoded inputs, we compute the final loss as: $\mathbf{l}_i = \texttt{MLP}_1(\hat{\mathbf{h}}_i)$, and $\mathbf{l}_a = \texttt{MLP}_1(\hat{\mathbf{h}}_a)$ and $\mathcal{L} = \alpha \times \mathcal{L}_i + \beta \times \mathcal{L}_a$, where $\mathbf{l}_i, \mathbf{l}_a$ represent the logits from $\hat{\mathbf{h}}_i$ and $\hat{\mathbf{h}}_a$ respectively, and $\mathcal{L}_i$ and $\mathcal{L}_a$ are their corresponding cross-entropy losses. α and β are hyperparameters that decide the contribution of the generated influence graphs and the procedural text to the loss. We set $\alpha = 1$ and $\beta = 0.9$ across experiments.

QA Evaluation Results Table 8 shows the accuracy of our method vs. the vanilla WIQA-BERT model by question type and number of hops between c and e. We also observe from Table 8 that augmenting the context with generated influences from CURIE leads to considerable gains over WIQA-BERT based model, with the largest improvement seen in 3-hop questions (questions where the e and c are at a distance of three reasoning hops in the influence graphs). The strong performance on the 3-hop question supports our hypothesis that generated influences might be able to connect two event influences that are farther apart in the reasoning chain. We also show in Table 8 that augmenting with CURIE improves performance on the difficult

Query Type	WIQA-BERT + CURIE	WIQA-BERT
1-hop	**78.78**	71.60
2-hop	**63.49**	62.50
3-hop	**68.28**	59.50
Out-of-para	**64.04**	56.13
In-para	73.58	**79.68**
No effect	**90.84**	89.38
Overall	**76.92**	73.80

Table 8: QA accuracy by number of hops, and question type. WIQA-BERT refers to the original WIQA-BERT results reported in Tandon et al. (2019), and WIQA-BERT + CURIE are the results obtained by augmenting the QA dataset with the influences generated by CURIE.

Out-of-para category of questions, which requires background knowledge.

Source of improved performance: *st* graphs? Since CURIE uses GPT-2 model to generate the graphs, we perform an additional experiment to verify whether simply using GPT-2 classifier for WIQA would achieve the same performance gains. To establish this, we train a GPT-2 classifier, and augment it with CURIE graphs to compare their relative performances on WIQA. Table 9 shows that augmenting CURIE graphs to both WIQA-BERT and GPT-2 classifiers provides consistent gains, suggesting the effectiveness of CURIE graphs.

Model	Accuracy
WIQA-BERT	73.80
WIQA-BERT + CURIE	**76.92***
GPT-2	72.70
GPT-2 + CURIE	**74.33***

Table 9: WIQA-QA results for both WIQA-BERT and GPT-2 augmented with CURIE graphs. Across both classifiers, augmenting CURIE graphs shows performance gains. *-indicates statistical significance

WIQA-BERT scores are slightly lower than the GPT-2 scores for WIQA classification despite having similar parameter size. We hypothesize that this is due to the pretrained classification token ([CLS]) in WIQA-BERT, while GPT-2 uses the pooling operation over the sequence for classification. In summary, the evaluation highlights the value of CURIE as a framework for improving performance on downstream tasks that require counterfactual reasoning and serves as an evaluation of the ability of CURIE to reason about *st*-scenarios.

4.2 Discussion

In summary, we show substantial gains when a generated st-graph is fed as an additional input to the QA model. Our approach forces the model to reason about influences within a context, and then answer the question, which proves to be better than answering the questions directly.

5 Related Work

Language Models for Knowledge Generation: Using large scale neural networks to generate knowledge has been studied under various task settings (Sap et al., 2019; Bosselut et al., 2019; Shwartz et al., 2020; Bosselut et al., 2021; Malaviya et al., 2019). Another line of querying language models (LMs) aims to understand the type of knowledge LMs contain. Davison et al. (2019) explore whether BERT prefers true or fictitious statements over ConceptNet (Speer et al., 2017). Logan et al. (2019) observe that the LM over-generalize to produce wrong facts, while Kassner and Schütze (2019) show that negated facts are also considered valid in an LM.

Our work closely aligns with Tandon et al. (2019), Bosselut et al. (2019), and Bosselut et al. (2021). Compared to Bosselut et al. (2019), CURIE gives a method that can naturally incorporate context and reason about situation via hops and nature of the influence. Additionally, any node can be arbitrarily expanded via the iterative procedure, producing complete graphs for situations. We reformulate the task of studying event influence from a QA task (Tandon et al., 2019) to a generation task. Our framework is similar in spirit to Bosselut et al. (2019), but extend it for situational reasoning with LMs. Bosselut et al. (2021) aim to generate events that can aid commonsense tasks. In contrast, our focus is context-grounded *st* graph generation. To this end, our formulation includes multiple forward/backward reactions, imminent and eventual edges, and an algorithm to compile the individual nodes to a complete graph (Algorithm 1).

Situational reasoning : There has been immense interest in extracting event chains (as causal graphs) in stories and news corpora in both unsupervised (Chambers and Jurafsky, 2008) and supervised (Rudinger et al., 2015; Liu et al., 2018; Asghar, 2016; Dunietz et al., 2017; Nordon et al., 2019; Zhao et al., 2017) settings. Such approaches often depend on events that are explicitly mentioned in the input text, thereby unable to generate events beyond the input text.

Recently, there has been interest in *st* reasoning from a retrieval setting (Lin et al., 2019) and also generation setting, attributed partially to the rise of neural generation models (Yangfeng Ji and Celikyilmaz, 2020) as knowledge bases (Petroni et al., 2019; Roberts et al., 2020; Talmor et al., 2020; Shwartz et al., 2020; Sap et al., 2019). Qin et al. (2019) present generation models to generate the path from a counterfactual to an ending in a story. Current systems make some simplifying assumptions, e.g. that the ending is known. Multiple *st* (e.g., more sunlight, more pollution) can happen at the same time, and these systems can only handle one situation at a time. All of these systems assume that *st* happens once in a context. Our framework strengthens this line of work by not assuming that the ending is given during deductive *st* reasoning.

6 Conclusion

We present CURIE, a situational reasoning that: (i) is effective at generating *st*-reasoning graphs, validated by automated metrics and human evaluations, (ii) improves performance on two downstream tasks by simply augmenting their input with the generated *st* graphs. Further, our framework supports recursively querying for any node in the *st*-graph. Our future work is to design models that seek consistency, and study recursive *st*-reasoning as a bridge between dialog and reasoning.

Acknowledgments

We would like to thank Peter Clark for the thoughtful discussions and useful feedback on the draft. We also want to thank the anonymous reviewers for valuable feedback. This material is partly based on research sponsored in part by the Air Force Research Laboratory under agreement number FA8750-19-2-0200. The U.S. Government is authorized to reproduce and distribute reprints for Governmental purposes notwithstanding any copyright notation thereon. The views and conclusions contained herein are those of the authors and should not be interpreted as necessarily representing the official policies or endorsements, either expressed or implied, of the Air Force Research Laboratory or the U.S. Government.

References

Nabiha Asghar. 2016. Automatic extraction of causal relations from natural language texts: A comprehensive survey. *ArXiv*, abs/1605.07895.

Dzmitry Bahdanau, Kyunghyun Cho, and Yoshua Bengio. 2015. Neural machine translation by jointly learning to align and translate. In *3rd International Conference on Learning Representations, ICLR 2015*.

Yonatan Bisk, Rowan Zellers, Ronan LeBras, Jianfeng Gao, and Yejin Choi. 2020. Piqa: Reasoning about physical commonsense in natural language. In *AAAI*, pages 7432–7439.

Antoine Bosselut, Ronan Le Bras, and Yejin Choi. 2021. Dynamic neuro-symbolic knowledge graph construction for zero-shot commonsense question answering. In *Proceedings of the 35th AAAI Conference on Artificial Intelligence (AAAI)*.

Antoine Bosselut, Hannah Rashkin, Maarten Sap, Chaitanya Malaviya, Asli Çelikyilmaz, and Yejin Choi. 2019. Comet: Commonsense transformers for automatic knowledge graph construction. In *ACL*.

Nathanael Chambers and Dan Jurafsky. 2008. Unsupervised learning of narrative event chains. In *Proceedings of ACL-08: HLT*, pages 789–797, Columbus, Ohio. Association for Computational Linguistics.

Joe Davison, Joshua Feldman, and Alexander Rush. 2019. Commonsense knowledge mining from pretrained models. In *Proceedings of the 2019 Conference on Empirical Methods in Natural Language Processing and the 9th International Joint Conference on Natural Language Processing (EMNLP-IJCNLP)*, pages 1173–1178, Hong Kong, China. Association for Computational Linguistics.

Jacob Devlin, Ming-Wei Chang, Kenton Lee, and Kristina Toutanova. 2019. BERT: Pre-training of deep bidirectional transformers for language understanding. In *Proceedings of the 2019 Conference of the North American Chapter of the Association for Computational Linguistics: Human Language Technologies, Volume 1 (Long and Short Papers)*, pages 4171–4186, Minneapolis, Minnesota. Association for Computational Linguistics.

Jesse Dunietz, Lori S. Levin, and J. Carbonell. 2017. Automatically tagging constructions of causation and their slot-fillers. *Transactions of the Association for Computational Linguistics*, 5:117–133.

Joseph L Fleiss and Jacob Cohen. 1973. The equivalence of weighted kappa and the intraclass correlation coefficient as measures of reliability. *Educational and psychological measurement*, 33(3):613–619.

H. Grice. 1975. Logic and conversation syntax and semantics. In *Logic and conversation Syntax and Semantics*.

Suchin Gururangan, Ana Marasović, Swabha Swayamdipta, Kyle Lo, Iz Beltagy, Doug Downey, and Noah A Smith. 2020. Don't stop pretraining: Adapt language models to domains and tasks. *arXiv preprint arXiv:2004.10964*.

Sepp Hochreiter and Jürgen Schmidhuber. 1997. Long short-term memory. *Neural computation*, 9(8):1735–1780.

Ari Holtzman, Jan Buys, Li Du, Maxwell Forbes, and Yejin Choi. 2019. The curious case of neural text degeneration. *arXiv preprint arXiv:1904.09751*.

Nora Kassner and Hinrich Schütze. 2019. Negated lama: Birds cannot fly. *arXiv preprint arXiv:1911.03343*.

Diederik P Kingma and Jimmy Ba. 2014. Adam: A method for stochastic optimization. *arXiv preprint arXiv:1412.6980*.

Chin-Yew Lin. 2004. Rouge: A package for automatic evaluation of summaries. In *Text summarization branches out*, pages 74–81.

Kevin Lin, Oyvind Tafjord, Peter Clark, and Matt Gardner. 2019. Reasoning over paragraph effects in situations. In *MRQA@EMNLP*.

Fei Liu, Trevor Cohn, and Timothy Baldwin. 2018. Narrative modeling with memory chains and semantic supervision. In *Proceedings of the 56th Annual Meeting of the Association for Computational Linguistics (Volume 2: Short Papers)*, pages 278–284, Melbourne, Australia. Association for Computational Linguistics.

Robert Logan, Nelson F Liu, Matthew E Peters, Matt Gardner, and Sameer Singh. 2019. Barack's wife hillary: Using knowledge graphs for fact-aware language modeling. In *Proceedings of the 57th Annual Meeting of the Association for Computational Linguistics*, pages 5962–5971.

Minh-Thang Luong, Hieu Pham, and Christopher D Manning. 2015. Effective approaches to attention-based neural machine translation. In *Proceedings of the 2015 Conference on Empirical Methods in Natural Language Processing*, pages 1412–1421.

Chaitanya Malaviya, Chandra Bhagavatula, Antoine Bosselut, and Yejin Choi. 2019. Exploiting structural and semantic context for commonsense knowledge base completion. *arXiv preprint arXiv:1910.02915*.

Galia Nordon, Gideon Koren, Varda Shalev, Benny Kimelfeld, Uri Shalit, and Kira Radinsky. 2019. Building causal graphs from medical literature and electronic medical records. In *Proceedings of the AAAI Conference on Artificial Intelligence*, volume 33, pages 1102–1109.

Kishore Papineni, Salim Roukos, Todd Ward, and Wei-Jing Zhu. 2002. Bleu: a method for automatic evaluation of machine translation. In *Proceedings of the 40th annual meeting on association for computational linguistics*, pages 311–318. Association for Computational Linguistics.

Jeffrey Pennington, Richard Socher, and Christopher D. Manning. 2014. Glove: Global vectors for word representation. In *Empirical Methods in Natural Language Processing (EMNLP)*, pages 1532–1543.

Fabio Petroni, Tim Rocktäschel, Sebastian Riedel, Patrick Lewis, Anton Bakhtin, Yuxiang Wu, and Alexander Miller. 2019. Language models as knowledge bases? In *Proceedings of the 2019 Conference on Empirical Methods in Natural Language Processing and the 9th International Joint Conference on Natural Language Processing (EMNLP-IJCNLP)*, pages 2463–2473.

Lianhui Qin, Antoine Bosselut, Ari Holtzman, Chandra Bhagavatula, Elizabeth Clark, and Yejin Choi. 2019. Counterfactual story reasoning and generation. *EMNLP*.

Alec Radford, Karthik Narasimhan, Tim Salimans, and Ilya Sutskever. 2018. Improving language understanding by generative pre-training. *URL https://s3-us-west-2. amazonaws. com/openai-assets/researchcovers/languageunsupervised/language understanding paper. pdf.*

Alec Radford, Jeffrey Wu, Rewon Child, David Luan, Dario Amodei, and Ilya Sutskever. 2019. Language models are unsupervised multitask learners. *OpenAI Blog*, 1(8):9.

Adam Roberts, Colin Raffel, and Noam Shazeer. 2020. How much knowledge can you pack into the parameters of a language model? In *Proceedings of the 2020 Conference on Empirical Methods in Natural Language Processing (EMNLP)*, pages 5418–5426.

Rachel Rudinger, Pushpendre Rastogi, Francis Ferraro, and Benjamin Van Durme. 2015. Script induction as language modeling. In *Proceedings of the 2015 Conference on Empirical Methods in Natural Language Processing*, pages 1681–1686.

Rachel Rudinger, Vered Shwartz, Jena D. Hwang, Chandra Bhagavatula, Maxwell Forbes, Ronan Le Bras, Noah A. Smith, and Yejin Choi. 2020. Thinking like a skeptic: Defeasible inference in natural language. In *Findings of the Association for Computational Linguistics: EMNLP 2020*, pages 4661–4675, Online. Association for Computational Linguistics.

Maarten Sap, Ronan Le Bras, Emily Allaway, Chandra Bhagavatula, Nicholas Lourie, Hannah Rashkin, Brendan Roof, Noah A Smith, and Yejin Choi. 2019. Atomic: An atlas of machine commonsense for if-then reasoning. In *Proceedings of the AAAI Conference on Artificial Intelligence*, volume 33, pages 3027–3035.

Vered Shwartz, Peter West, Ronan Le Bras, Chandra Bhagavatula, and Yejin Choi. 2020. Unsupervised commonsense question answering with self-talk. In *Proceedings of the 2020 Conference on Empirical Methods in Natural Language Processing (EMNLP)*, pages 4615–4629.

Robyn Speer, Joshua Chin, and Catherine Havasi. 2017. Conceptnet 5.5: An open multilingual graph of general knowledge. In *Thirty-First AAAI Conference on Artificial Intelligence*.

Nitish Srivastava, Geoffrey Hinton, Alex Krizhevsky, Ilya Sutskever, and Ruslan Salakhutdinov. 2014. Dropout: a simple way to prevent neural networks from overfitting. *The journal of machine learning research*, 15(1):1929–1958.

Oyvind Tafjord, Peter Clark, Matt Gardner, Wen-tau Yih, and Ashish Sabharwal. 2019. Quarel: A dataset and models for answering questions about qualitative relationships. In *Proceedings of the AAAI Conference on Artificial Intelligence*, volume 33, pages 7063–7071.

Alon Talmor, Yanai Elazar, Yoav Goldberg, and Jonathan Berant. 2020. olmpics-on what language model pre-training captures. *Transactions of the Association for Computational Linguistics*, 8:743–758.

Niket Tandon, Bhavana Dalvi, Keisuke Sakaguchi, Peter Clark, and Antoine Bosselut. 2019. Wiqa: A dataset for "what if..." reasoning over procedural text. In *Proceedings of the 2019 Conference on Empirical Methods in Natural Language Processing and the 9th International Joint Conference on Natural Language Processing (EMNLP-IJCNLP)*, pages 6078–6087.

Thomas Wolf, L Debut, V Sanh, J Chaumond, C Delangue, A Moi, P Cistac, T Rault, R Louf, M Funtowicz, et al. 2019. Huggingface's transformers: State-of-the-art natural language processing. *ArXiv, abs/1910.03771*.

Thomas Wolf Yangfeng Ji, Antoine Bosselut and Asli Celikyilmaz. 2020. The amazing world of generation. *EMNLP tutorials*.

Sendong Zhao, Quan Wang, Sean Massung, Bing Qin, T. Liu, Bin Wang, and ChengXiang Zhai. 2017. Constructing and embedding abstract event causality networks from text snippets. *Proceedings of the Tenth ACM International Conference on Web Search and Data Mining*.

A Appendix

A.1 Polarity Words

To compute polarity for error analysis, we use the following words as guidelines.

Increasing words *helps, more, higher, increase, increases, stronger, faster, greater, longer, larger, helping*

Decreasing words *hurts, less, lower, decrease, decreases, weaker, slower, smaller, hurting, softer, fewer*

B Examples from CURIE

In table 12, we show some qualitative QA examples from CURIE. Here, *Topic Matches* signifies whether the generated answers is relevant to the context.

Path Length	Question	Answer	Predicted Answer	Topic Matches
2	hurts more magma is released	LESS igneous rock forming	LESS or SMALLER eruptions.	Yes
2	hurts more water in solid or liquid phase	MORE evaporation?	LESS vapor being made.	Yes
2	hurts less flowers for bees to visit	MORE flowers being pollinated?	a LARGER cake?.	No
1	helps changes in the atmosphere	if the moon orbits slower	MORE/LARGER solar power being generated?.	No
2	helps less time goes by	there are fewer fissures	LESS or SMALLER eruptions.	Yes
3	hurts there is less water in the lakes	a MORE INTENSE water cycle?	MORE salt being removed from the water.	No
2	helps tectonic plates rub less	SMALLER mountains	LESS or SMALLER eruptions.	Yes
1	hurts Better crop watering	LESS crops	LESS vegetables.	Yes
3	hurts weather is accommodating for frogs	LESS frogs	LESS or SMALLER Frogs.	Yes
1	helps there will be more eggs	MORE fish?	MORE birds.	No
3	helps Urine levels increase	LESS waste being removed from the body	MORE waste being removed from the body.	Yes
3	helps Having normal body functions	HURTING the DNA to replicate properly	MORE cells being damaged.	Yes
2	helps not having a water source nearby	vines will grow faster	LESS or SMALLER grapes.	Yes
1	hurts bees may become extinct	more bees are collecting pollen	LESS butterflies.	Yes
3	hurts more bees fly around	LESS flowers being pollinated	a SMALLER flowers.	Yes
2	hurts the earths core gets warmer	less volcanic mountains are formed	LESS or SMALLER valleys being formed.	Yes
3	hurts more land available	LESS igneous rock forming	less magma cools.	Yes
3	hurts there is less water on the ground	a MORE INTENSE water cycle	MORE salt being removed from the water.	No

Table 10: Sample Generations. Topic matches captures whether the topic of the generated event matches with the context. (section 3). Path length = 1 refers to the immediate effects, and Path length > 1 refers to eventual effects.

Path Length	Question	Answer	Predicted Answer	Topic Matches
3	hurts more conservation achieved	LESS flowers being pollinated	less nectar available.	Yes
2	hurts the eggs become food for other fish	MORE fish	Less larvae eat and grow.	Yes
2	helps more magma inside volcano	more magma changes in pressure	MORE/GREATER eruptions?.	Yes
2	helps less commercial fishing	more fry emerge	LESS damage by acid rain.	
2	hurts more stormy weather occurs	less plant growth occurs	MORE vegetables.	Yes
2	helps more pumpkin seeds planted	MORE or LARGER pumpkins	more water used for more flowers.	No
2	hurts more Global warming causes extreme temperatures	Rains are plentiful and more regular	MORE vegetables?.	Yes
2	helps warmer weather evaporates more water	a MORE INTENSE water cycle	MORE/STRONGER storms?.	Yes
2	helps dry hot environment evaporates water	LESS frogs	MORE or LARGER frogs.	Yes
3	helps stronger heat source	MORE evaporation	more heat causes the molecules to increase in energy.	Yes
2	helps living in a rain forest	more water collects in the bodies of water	MORE salt being removed from the water.	No
2	hurts there is no tadpole from the egg	MORE frogs	MORE ELABORATE swimming.	No
1	helps more pulling and stretching of tetonic plates	more cracks in earths crust	MORE or STRONGER earthquakes.	Yes
2	hurts less animals that hunt frogs	less tadpoles loses their tails	more fish grow bigger.	No
2	hurts both kidneys are present and functioning	less waste is removed from the blood	less waste is removed in the blood.	Yes

Table 11: Sample Generations. Topic matches captures whether the topic of the generated event matches with the context. (section 3). Path length = 1 refers to the immediate effects, and Path length > 1 refers to eventual effects. (section 3).

Path Length	Question	Answer	Predicted Answer	Topic Matches
2	helps the bees have a very hairy leg gene	the bees would carry more pollen away from the flower	a LARGER nectar star.	Yes
2	hurts If more eggs are layed	MORE frogs	the mouth will grow smaller.	No
1	hurts bees are imported	fewer bees land on flowers	a SMALLER hive.	No
1	hurts more adolescent fish grow to adulthood	fewer fish can lay more eggs	LESS damage by acid rain.	No
2	helps the heat rises	greater precipitations will happen	MORE/STRONGER .	Yes
2	helps All the eggs were eaten	There were few eggs laid	less eggs are laid..	Yes
1	hurts plates move away from each other	edges of plates crumple more	MORE or GREATER eruptions.	Yes
1	hurts more proteins available	less help occurs	less endowment of nucleotides.	Yes

Table 12: Sample Generations. Topic matches captures whether the topic of the generated event matches with the context. Path length = 1 refers to the immediate effects, and Path length > 1 refers to eventual effects. (section 3).

Author Index

Aglionby, Guy, 1

Baldwin, Timothy, 8
Broniatowski, David A., 43

Chang, Shih-Fu, 23
Clark, Peter, 49
Cong, Yan, 17

Diab, Mona, 43

Hosseini, Pedram, 43
Hovy, Eduard H, 49

Koto, Fajri, 8

Lau, Jey Han, 8

Ma, Yueen, 23
Madaan, Aman, 49

Nguyen, Tuan-Phong, 36

Prabhumoye, Shrimai, 49

Rajagopal, Dheeraj, 49
Ravichander, Abhilasha, 49
Razniewski, Simon, 36

Tandon, Niket, 49
Tuefel, Simone, 1

Wan, Yue, 23
Wang, Zhecan, 23

Yang, Yiming, 49
You, Haoxuan, 23

Association for Computational Linguistics
209 N. Eighth Street
Stroudsburg, Pennsylvania 18360

ISBN 978-1-7138-6732-6

CURRAN ASSOCIATES INC.
proceedings.com